Ladies, Front & Center!

Elevate Humanity Through
Self Discovery

MELVIN ANDERSON

Ladies, Front & Center!
Elevate Humanity Through Self Discovery
by Melvin Anderson

Published by:
See It Through Publishing, Inc.
Atlanta, Georgia 30339
Contact@SeeItThroughPublishing.com

Printed on 100% recycled paper in the United States of America

ISBN 978-0-615-46592-0

FIRST EDITION: December 2011
10 9 8 7 6 5 4 3 2 1

Ladies, Front & Center! books are available at quantity discounts when utilized to promote products or services. Please visit the following website:

www.LadiesFrontAndCenter.net

To each person that offered support:

THANK YOU!

Acknowledgements

To My Wife

To My Mother

Two Women Full of Love, Wisdom, Knowledge,

Balance and Unwavering Strength.

I Love You and Thank You!

Introduction

Try to imagine a time when you simply purchase a newspaper and it is a normal occurrence to read a number of articles detailing recent success stories and breaking discoveries concerning the wellbeing of people throughout this world. For example, "Child Poverty Reduced 72% Throughout the World" or "Inventor Develops Solution to Eradicate Homelessness." Or "Genocide No Longer a Concern in a Number of Countries," "Global Peace Summit Reaches 90% of Goals" or one of my favorite headlines "Female Leaders of the Seven Largest Countries Balance Federal Budgets in Record Time." Yes, I am somewhat a dreamer, and yes, I truly believe that these types of scenarios are obtainable and can become daily occurrences for all mankind. Fortunately, there are many dreamers today that are doing their part to discover global solutions. As individuals, we must constantly ask ourselves how we can make a difference. This book is one of my efforts to possibly make a difference and contribute to the overall good of humans. In order to make a difference in today's environment, a person must determine how he/she can help, develop a plan and implement. Problem, solution, action! Of course, our individual contribution to the world does not have to be a daunting task. It can be something quite simple, such as informing a child that their potential is endless and they can accomplish anything in life with a little effort. This small gesture contributes to the global effort of solving problems.

No Warm and Fuzzy Here!

I must inform you that this is not a feel good/entertaining/cuddly type of book. There is no Hollywood love story with a knight in shining armor or a number of soft stories that will cause you to cry. Not in this book! Quite the opposite. This book requires the reader to first expand his/her thinking and from that point, roll up his/her sleeves for a reflective workout. The chapters are not arranged to be read in a sequential order; certain chapters may not be applicable or offer no interest to you. I suggest that you begin by reviewing the table of contents and select three to four chapters that pique your interest. Then cover the remaining chapters at your leisure.

My desire is for this content to challenge each of you to love yourself, trust yourself, elevate yourself, improve yourself, educate yourself and then share yourself with the world and bless us all. This work is applicable to every woman on this beautiful planet regardless of race, creed, color, or religion/belief system. This journey requires work, discipline, openness and patience, but I promise you that it will be well worth the effort. You are a woman! Need I say more?

Now let's get to the questions that you are asking concerning this book. 1) Why did I choose women as my target audience and 2) who in the hell classified this man as an expert on subjects concerning women? Great questions! As a matter of fact, as I was writing this book, I conducted a number of surveys with women concerning the content. I actually had one woman respond with the following comment: "I would never read a book written by a man entitled Ladies, Front & Center!" Point well taken.

Let's address the latter question first. I clearly remember the day that I talked with my wife concerning writing this book. She only had one question: What the hell do you know about women? From that moment, we never discussed the subject and she was unaware of my efforts until I recently presented a copy of the manuscript. As my wife eloquently pointed out, I do not consider myself an expert on women or any of the subjects of this book. I made it a point to create separation between the true scholars and myself. I do not consider myself an expert, and I do not have the credentials to provide answers or solid research data concerning the subject matter of each chapter. What you will notice is that throughout the book, I simply ask questions. The responses to my questions are a collection of proven data gathered by a number of leading scholars in their particular field. Each scholar listed in this book has conducted extensive research to validate their data. This is the reason that I was comfortable gathering data and presenting to my audience.

Why did I select women as the target subject? This answer is quite simple. In my humble opinion, women are better equipped to achieve global results than men. In addition, I talked with a number of individuals that conduct programs for troubled youth and I asked two questions: How important is it for a mother to possess inner strength/beauty and also display this strength in her children's presence? Would this, at any level, help the child? The answer: an overwhelming YES! Women hold the power of creation, women are the mothers of our children, women are the nurturers, women naturally offer balance, and a woman's womb is the creation of all life and often comparable to a sanctuary. Women get the job done! Yes, as a man, I said it and I fully support my statement. I might be removed from the male team; however, there has been an awakening among women and their daughters, and men are fortunate to witness this transformation.

Ladies, Front & Center! is simply a book that offers insight into the possibility of elevating humanity utilizing substantiated methods researched by renowned social scientists and scholars. I simply asked myself two simple questions: How can we elevate humanity? What can I do to help? The content of this book is just one of the many ways that I have chosen to attempt to make a difference. I have always believed in the phrase "Each one teach one" and have lived my life implementing this belief. If any part of the content of this book provides just a small glimpse of enlightenment, I am truly grateful, and my efforts completing this book were well worth the time.

For a number of years I have been quite discouraged by the current state of the human species. For a species that strongly believes in a higher power, our actions are quite the opposite of our so called belief systems. Children and adults are homeless, starving and dying daily; humans kill humans based solely upon fundamental differences in belief systems or greed; education systems are a failure in many countries; and there is hatred/violence toward people of different physical features. At this moment in time, I question the overall intelligence of our species.

Finding a Man

This book is void of any content in reference to relationships, such as how to find a man, how to meet a man, how to keep a man, or how to cook for a man. The absence of this type of information might be disappointing to some. For example, during a survey with a lady concerning the subjects of each chapter, she asked if there were going to be any chapters in reference to relationships with men. I answered no and she stated that the book was not worth reading if it did not include content pertaining to the role of a man in a woman's life. Her final comment was this: There is no discussion of the self discovery of a woman without a man. As you might have determined, this woman was very traditional. She believed that her role in life was to take care of a man, and her life was not complete without this activity. Contrary to this belief, there are many women that have discovered that it is extremely important to work on themselves before bringing others into the picture. This project is strictly about each woman discovering herself and simply conveying a number of subjects that have been proven to move you closer to self-discovery. I strongly believe - and many scholars have proven - that it is difficult to attract the right mate when a person has not discovered their inner beauty and strength. A person must learn to love themselves, believe in themselves, and seek inner peace. In addition, I strongly believe that when a person seeks improvement within, this process creates a positive energy that will attract individuals with similar energy patterns. I am not stating that I believe that men are not important in the lives of women or that a woman does not need a man or partner. Quite the opposite! This particular project, however, was written primarily to identify a number of proven strategies that might assist others to seek power within.

Seek Within

If the woman is to reach heights unknown, what are some of the attributes required to at least begin the process? Simple – a woman must first believe in herself. A woman must first love herself. A woman must first recognize her value and worth. A woman must first desire to seek knowledge and wisdom. Truly believing the above statements, the content of this book was assembled. I hope that you will discover its value.

Culinary Expressions

In the beginning of each chapter, you will notice that the first two pages consist of dialogue between two or more individuals addressing a real world situation consistent with the subject matter of that particular chapter.

The reason behind this method is to 1) provide the reader with an idea of the chapter content and 2) briefly break up the seriousness of the content by integrating food into the content. Within the content of each conversation, I made a point to have the individuals enjoying a particular type of cuisine while discussing their individual subject matter. For example, in chapter four, there is a conversation that includes a mother, father and their adult daughter. The conversation occurs in their gourmet kitchen, where the father is preparing a wonderful breakfast for his family. I made a point to utilize a different cuisine for each chapter, along with carefully selected menu items which correlate to the personalities and relationships of the participants. Quite frankly, the descriptions might actually bring about a craving while reading.

Contents

CHAPTER EIGHT • 189

Men are Idiots!

Chapter One

The History of the Matter

Critical Thinking

"Good evening, ladies. Are we ready to order?" asks the waiter.

"Yes," the ladies respond in unison.

"OK, what will it be this evening?" asks the waiter.

Sheila responds, "I will have the red-wine braised Wild Alaskan Salmon with shiitake mushrooms with a truffled herb salad."

Tasha responds, "I think I will start with the Sautéed Calamari and for my entrée, I will have the English-Cut Lamb Chop along with roasted asparagus."

"Great, ladies. I will get your drinks and your orders will be out shortly."

"Thank you, Lance," responds Tasha.

"My pleasure," responds the waiter.

"So Sheila, how have you been? It has been more than a year since we've had a chance to spend some time together. How are you doing? What has been keeping you so busy?"

"Well it has been a while." responds Sheila. "All is well on my end. I've finally made some tough decisions about my life, and I am moving forward with a solid plan. And one of those plans is that I am launching a business that sells cherry pies to consumers, bakeries and restaurants."

"That is great!" responds Tasha. "Tell me about this venture. I am excited for you!"

Sheila responds "Well it all started when I visited my grandmother about a year ago. I was taking some time to reflect on my life and felt the best place to do that was in her presence. We are very close, and I truly respect her thoughts and strength. Well, one evening after dinner, we sat in front of a nice fire in her living room and we enjoyed a slightly warm slice of this delicious cherry pie. The second that I tasted this cherry pie, I knew that it was something special. I mean the crust was perfect and the flavor of the cherries and the filling just brought joy to my mouth. I asked her why she never baked this pie for our family. She stated that she stopped making her cherry pie years before my birth because of an incident in her past. She explained that the last time that she baked that particular recipe was the night before my grandfather passed. She stated that her cherry pie was grandpa's favorite dessert and once a month, they would sit in front of that old fireplace and enjoy not only the cherry pie but also each other's company. She said that sometimes they would sit and just gaze at each other as grandpa would feed her this delicious dessert. That event was so important to her that it became an emotional issue each time she baked that pie after his death. So she never baked that cherry pie until that day she and I were together. It has been over thirty years. She said that she needed closure and that night was great healing for both of us."

"That story is truly amazing!" says Tasha.

"Yes it was!" says Sheila. "So to honor her, and of course since the cherry pie was so delicious, I asked her if I could possibly sell the cherry pie to the world. She said yes and gave me the recipe. So I am launching this business to share my grandmother's energy with the world. I think that this cherry pie is the best in the world. Everyone will enjoy this pie."

Tasha responds "That is great, Sheila. Now let me ask one question. Have you taken the time to taste other cherry pies just for comparison?" asks Tasha. "Have you tasted a cherry pie made in San Francisco, Paris, New Zealand? Have you studied the history of this particular dessert? Who made the first cherry pie? Where did it originate? What were the circumstances surrounding this creation? What ingredients did they use at that particular time? How did this recipe evolve over time? Where did your grandmother get her inspiration behind her recipe? I ask these questions for this reason. One of my mentors would always say to me, 'Find the history of the matter'. And I did not understand his statement until I put it to task. What I discovered is that when you take the time to gather as much information as possible concerning your subject, you infuse your subject with the energy of others, which helps you to enhance the value of that subject. When you research the history of the cherry pie and travel the world to experience cherry pies from different countries, cities and small villages, your experiences will provide you with ideas that will enhance your grandmother's recipe and connect you with the past of that delicious dessert."

"Wow that makes perfect sense," responds Sheila. "I really feel that your feedback will make a huge difference in the operation of this business. Tasha, thank you for your advice."

"Sheila, you are more than welcome. Anything that I can do to make your venture a success, I will be there for you. Now let's try this restaurant's cherry pie and gather some market research."

Many of us journey through life making important decisions based solely on limited data or our own life experiences. For the most part, we are more inclined to rely upon our own belief systems or information commonly amassed from our inner circle, such as family and friends. Fortunately, for a number of our decisions, an extended knowledge base is not required; however, each one of us has experienced situations in which additional information would have been helpful. Wouldn't it be outstanding if we were fortunate to have individuals in our inner circle that are subject matter experts when facing life situations? I wish that each one of us could be so fortunate. Fortunately, there are many experts outside of our individual circles with a number of tools, methods and processes at their disposal willing to share their findings with us.

One of the most important processes when evaluating circumstances is to gather as much subject data as possible. A wealth of information leads to sound decisions. One of the critical components of information gathering is to understand the history of any subject matter. Unfortunately, we rarely seek information that taps into the history or background of a particular subject. We rarely ask the question, "What is the history of this particular subject?" or as I phrase it, the history of the matter. When I speak of "the history of the matter," I am speaking of just one of the fundamental processes of critical thinking – a process which enlightens your path of discovery by enhancing your ability to thoroughly evaluate a subject matter. The subject matter can be an idea, work or personal project, life situation, or the launching of a business. Any situation in life can be applicable to this process.

Even though I have always been a person who constantly asks questions pertaining to various subjects, I was lacking a process that offered a systematic approach to gathering needed data and the ability to evaluate and categorize that data to make it even more useful. The critical thinking process allowed me to expand my reasoning and decision making skills proficiency, and one of the most helpful components of critical thinking was the "history of the matter." Introduced to me over a decade ago by a mentor, this component has been one of the most important tools discovered for me in my lifetime. What is this process of discovering the history of a matter?

Before we discuss the process, please allow me to give you a little history concerning my mentor. Throughout my life, I have made it a point to sit with masters of various disciplines, individuals passionate with sharing their knowledge with others. One of those individuals is a gentleman and friend that I have had the pleasure of knowing for more than fifteen years, Mr. Ken Krautter. A humble man with humble beginnings, this man has a huge heart and has dedicated his life to the betterment of man. During the first few years of our mentor sessions, we would meet for breakfast at a local hotel at a minimum of twice per month. The hotel was a small, quiet facility with an agreeable breakfast buffet. An early riser, Mr. Krautter would arrive at the hotel promptly at 6 a.m., armed with a number of local and national newspapers, waiting for my 7 a.m. arrival.

Now, back to the explanation of Mr. Krautter's "history of the matter" process. There are two stages that provide the framework. The first stage focuses strictly on mastering the skills required to discover, or "open your eyes" to, additional information of a particular subject which provides a deeper understanding of the subject. The second stage consists of real world implementation of your training on a particular subject or project. Let's examine how he introduced this process to me.

The first stage began with just a little homework. Mr. Krautter selected an article from a specific newspaper and instructed me to read the article at that moment. As I mentioned earlier, Mr. Krautter begins his day by reading a number of local and national newspapers, such as The Atlanta Journal and Constitution, USA Today, Washington Post, or New York Times, to name a few. After I completed reading the article, he would ask probing questions concerning the subject matter of the article simply to determine if I had at least a basic understanding of the content. If so, I was asked to explain my interpretation. Of course with my somewhat arrogant attitude, I would always assume that I understood the content and the writer's intent for the article. The majority of the time, I was able to explain my initial interpretation of the article; however, his intent was for me to be able to examine the article a little closer, review each sentence and ask if there could be additional meaning. He expressed that there is always additional information concerning any subject matter if you are able to further analyze the content.

After I read the article, he would ask, "So, what do you think?" At that point, I would begin to give my explanation of what the writer was trying to get across to the reader. He would then continue with a minimum of three additional questions specifically linked to my prior response. That's when the fun began. From that point forward, he would ask his patented probing questions, which were totally unrelated to the perceived objective of the article. He would pull back the curtain of the article to evaluate what he referred to as the hidden content of the subject. Each time, his questions actually bordered upon irrelevance, but always seemed to reveal itself as the opposite. Mr. Krautter would ask, "What is the history of the writer? What is the primary subject matter of the article? What beliefs does he/she represent? What organizations is that individual associated with? What other articles has he/she written and under what news platform? Which newspapers/magazines does he/she write for, and what is the history of the newspaper and its ownership? Great questions to ask when seeking additional insight of any subject matter.

Immediately, I assumed that this information gathering would require an enormous amount of time, but I quickly learned that gathering that information was seamless and did not require a lot of time. Locating the answers to these types of questions was quite simple and required a small amount of time because of technology. Tools available on-line provided the means to gather detailed information concerning a number of subjects. For example, if you are preparing a presentation for a company, the company's website provides a wealth of information concerning their history, culture, mission, products, management, etc. In addition, if the company is a public company, the company is required to file SEC annual and quarterly reports which provide the majority of information needed to complete the proposal. If you are developing a plan, a wealth of information is at your disposal with little effort.

I quickly realized the importance of this process. After answering those types of questions, re-reading the article revealed an entirely different outlook and meaning. It was like I was reading the article for the first time. I was recognizing certain words and phrases that presented a different outlook and tone compared to my first reading. I immediately realized the value of this methodology; this process would be applicable throughout my life's journey. Mr. Krautter helped me in a way that will always allow me to tap into a wealth of information for every situation that I would face. Implementing this discipline would eliminate a number of barriers and answer many questions. It was truly an enlightening experience.

After six months of evaluating articles from a number of newspapers and news magazines, we moved to the second stage. This particular stage would focus on a real world implementation of his teachings of my choosing. I selected a proposal that I was presenting to a Fortune 500 company. The proposal consisted of offering services to develop a computer based employee training solution to increase efficiency along with reducing time, resources and cost. Yes, this was a while ago.

To begin the process, Mr. Krautter requested that I provide a thorough understanding of my business. What is my business? What do I offer as a product/service? At his request, I presented a copy of my business and marketing plan for his review. Once he completed the evaluation of the plan, he demanded a role play session in which I would conduct the presentation that I would present to a potential customer. During this presentation, his role was to act as the customer and ask a few general questions to complete his understanding of my business and as you can guess, his questions were quite informative. Together, we began the evaluation process of the proposal.

At that time, my business was based upon obtaining consulting fees for developing computer based training software for Fortune 1000 companies. One of the initial processes of my sales and marketing plan required me to contact and schedule presentations with key members of training departments which handled the corresponding budgets and responsibilities for this type of service. My strategy was simple: schedule a presentation with a senior member of the training team, conduct a thorough presentation, demonstrate sample projects from other customers, address any questions, close the meeting and follow up at a later date. Mr. Krautter didn't see it as being that simple. He began his patented probing process.

In my proposal, I provided information concerning my services, experience, and cost/budget breakdown. I also provided return on investment (ROI) data, support options, schematics, project time lines, deliverables, etc. I was thorough in detailing my project deliverables. He began by asking one simple question. "When and where was the Fortune 500 corporation founded?" And I thought to myself, Why is that information important? He began to explain. It is important to understand the history and culture of any company that you target. After reflecting on his comments, I recalled a situation in which his method was proven. It was a situation in which I scheduled an initial meeting with a company to introduce my services. On the day of the presentation, I approached the primary reception area, registered and received a security badge. The company required that an employee accompany any guest when in their building. The gentleman was called, and he met me in the lobby. We began to walk toward the elevators with the standard introductory conversation discussing the weather, work schedules, etc. Once we entered the elevator, the gentleman offered a small suggestion: "Let me advise you that on your next visit to our corporate office, it might be wise not to wear a blue tie. You might want to invest in a red tie since our corporate colors are red and white. Blue is the color of our primary competitor." Seemingly an insignificant detail, the corporate colors were extremely important to the company and its employees. At that time, if I had understood the importance of researching the history of the matter, I would not have missed that simple element.

Next question: "Do you have an understanding of the company's overall business?" Even though my services were applicable to only a small segment of the company's business, Mr. Krautter stressed that it would be in my best interest to also understand the company's overall offerings or core products/services. Keep in mind that this critical thinking process is applicable to any subject matter. Let's imagine that you are searching for a noteworthy private school for your child. One of the first things that you would most likely arrange is conversations with friends or family who are familiar with the school. This is considered an initial step of utilizing critical thinking. Your friends provide raving reviews concerning this school and their responses initialized further questions that can only be answered by the administration of the school. What is the history of the school? When was it founded? By what individual(s) or entity? What are the beliefs or standards of the founding individual(s)? What other type of projects have they been involved in before creating the school? Who are the largest financial donors/supporters? What other causes do the donors provide financial support? These types of questions reveal the core belief/value system of the founders which most likely will represent the content and values of that particular school. This type of information gathering is extremely important when evaluating situations throughout your life and produces tremendous results.

The Importance of Understanding History in General

The understanding of the history of any matter begins with the fundamental respect of history itself, primarily your history. This can be the history of your family, culture, country, people, etc. An understanding of this history is the foundation of any journey and reveals much about ourselves and our future. Where did your family originate? Within your particular group, what was their culture in earlier centuries? How much of your ancestors' history is part of your life? What did they learn which will benefit you today and your children in the future? Answering these types of questions will undoubtedly provide vital information, such as addressing a specific issue or developing a plan of action. For example, breast cancer is a major problem today among women. It is occurring at alarming rates and has affected relatives within my family as well as my wife's family. One of the preventive methods is to determine the history of breast cancer in your family.

When you accept the task of understanding your history, the information obtained from this process enhances your connection to your inner group, clarifies the importance of a connection to other groups, and eventually creates overall change in your decision making and thinking. For example, if your passion is to become an Italian chef, by simply researching the history of the Italian culture and cuisine, you immediately improve your skill set by arming yourself with beneficial data. From that moment forward, an appreciation of that particular history will become a part of your preparation, cooking and presentation, enhancing your craft and leading to a more fulfilling career.

Importance of Critical Thinking

What is this thing called critical thinking? It seems as if it is a complicated subject. Not at all. As a matter of fact, each person utilizes a part of critical thinking daily. For example, there is a young lady on a date with a gentleman for the first time. The first date is usually a fact finding mission, probing to learn more about her date. As the appetizers are being served, she begins to ask questions. "What characteristics define your woman of choice?" The gentleman expresses that he is searching for a companion that is independent, determined in her career path, and confident in herself spiritually, physically and mentally. His date immediately acknowledges and approves of his response. Her interest is piqued because he has referenced a number of qualities that she possesses; however, she is a critical thinker and would like to verify his statement. She begins to inquire about his history: Tell me about your relationship with your mother. What were some of the issues with a possible past mate? What are your beliefs in reference to the role of a woman in a relationship? Being able to logically evaluate his responses eventually leads to clarity which confirms or disputes his earlier response. She will reach a conclusion that is supported by a wealth of data based upon simply asking detailed questions.

Critical thinking is crucial when facing life's challenges or developing the next biggest idea. By walking through simple steps and asking yourself a variety of questions, you begin to understand your subject matter more thoroughly, leading to sound decisions. Critical thinking applies to all situations we face, such as raising children, getting out of debt, addressing a project at work, marriage and even implementing a business idea. Understanding this particular discipline will become an important component.

Let's take a moment to examine the definition of critical thinking. As stated by the National Council for Excellence in Critical Thinking (Paul, Elder), critical thinking is defined as "the intellectually disciplined process of actively and skillfully conceptualizing, applying, analyzing, synthesizing, and/or evaluating information gathered from, or generated by, observation, experience, reflection, reasoning, or communication, as a guide to belief and action." It is based on universal intellectual values that transcend subject matter divisions: clarity, accuracy, precision, consistency, relevance, sound evidence, good reasons, depth, breadth, and fairness. Simply stated, critical thinking is self-directed, self-disciplined, self-monitored, and self-corrective thinking. Dr. Richard Paul, founder of the Council, framed critical thinking as "thinking about your thinking while you're thinking in order to make your thinking better."

Unfortunately, it may seem that this subject matter is primarily intended for researchers and Ph.D.s; however these tools can be utilized by any individual throughout their life.

What is the purpose of understanding critical thinking? To begin, for many individuals, our present thinking is obscured by various forms of distorted and uninformed information. We are constantly inundated with massive levels of information, which can be overwhelming for many. We become cluttered in our thinking, which leads to a lack of basic understanding of many subjects. Studies (Paul) have revealed that with poor thinking, time and energy is wasted, which can affect our quality of life. Critical thinking can clear the path of confusion in order to reach logical solutions. As Richard Paul stated, "Critical thinking is not just thinking, but thinking which entails self-improvement."

Development of Your Critical Thinking Skills

How do we develop our critical thinking? We must realize that all humans possess critical thinking skills and have the capacity to develop those skills. I cannot stress this point enough. No person should believe that they are incapable of developing these types of skills so we must begin the development process. For example, one method utilized to develop critical thinking is to simply include someone in your inner circle that 1) doesn't constantly agree with you and 2) challenges your belief system. Each one of us should include someone in our circle that is not apprehensive when expressing different opinions and also unwilling to merely agree with you based upon your friendship-someone who offers constant challenge. This consistent process will lead to self improvement by forcing you to examine your belief system along with learning of other systems.

After learning of this strategy, I thought it might be interesting to test this method among friends. Unaware of my plan, I selected three intelligent and professional individuals within my circle that offered expertise on a number of subject matters. Once I defined the subjects, I developed a six month strategy consisting of 1) purposely initiating conversations that offered opinions opposing their way of thinking or belief systems and 2) engaging in their conversations and introducing responses that would mildly challenge or even discount their statements or conclusions, leading to quite interesting conversations.

To provide a brief description of my good friends, they happen to be three male professionals in senior management positions of Fortune 100 companies. We are all of a similar age group and members of the same fraternity. I have had the privilege of knowing these gentlemen for a decade and have spent a lot of time with this group.

They are individuals with a wealth of operations, management, and sales experience along with highly creative ideas. Each person shares similar experiences and ideas concerning life processes, career interests and advanced business principles. Of course, I cannot exclude the fact that each one of us possesses a slightly elevated ego. We would frequently get together for a drink or two while either watching a sporting event, brainstorming about a business idea, or talking jobs, politics, news or any other subject of interest. When I first met these guys and after a few months of "hanging with the bruhs", I began to notice that even though there were subjects upon which we would disagree, we consciously made an effort not to agitate or bruise egos. I labeled this process as the "Masters of the Universe Syndrome." We were constantly praising each other's opinions and beliefs without pushing the envelope to induce deeper thinking. This was a perfect scenario to implement my plan.

The first test occurred when one of the guys was sharing a situation in which the three of them launched a company that provided engineering, financial and management services to high net worth individuals, specifically residential construction management. This particular job consisted of managing the construction of a $1 million home. To make a long story short, their services were beneficial and saved the customer over $50,000 on construction costs and also completed construction one month before the deadline. Job well done and actually quite impressive! They developed a plan, implemented the plan and delivered positive results for their customer. As they were sharing their experience, they were, of course, praising each other as if they recently discovered the atom, which was the ideal time to launch my experiment. I congratulated the team and simply asked one simple question: "Great job, guys. Now, how many jobs did your team close after this project?" The answer was zero. Then I asked, "Did you form a corporation to offer these types of services or was this a specific service offered to a friend?" They actually formed a corporation. Next question, "When did you complete this particular project?" Response: Over three years prior.

Now the fun began. "Well, what in the hell happened? Why are you guys sitting here three years later boasting about this one job? From where I am sitting, your business failed because you were unable to close any other deals beyond the first. Please place your egos back into your pocket." Needless to say, they did not take my comment very well, which lead to an hour of dialogue, debating and ego protecting. I was instantly branded as a trouble maker, as well as an arrogant ass/know-it-all. What an experience! Highly entertaining and quite useful. Able to capture out-of-the-box responses from a group of highly skilled corporate professionals provided a wealth of data. I continued my research for six months.

After the six month period of observation of the group, I must say that I was somewhat surprised of the results. In addition, the process actually affected our individual relationships. Out of the three individuals, my relationship/friendship with two of the individuals has changed to the point of literally altering our communication pattern. The remaining individual actually recognized value in the process. This gentleman happens to be an individual that constantly seeks a challenge and embraces the notion of thinking outside of the box. At one point, I talked with each gentleman separately explaining my case study and to my surprise, the feedback was quite inspiring. As a matter of fact, one individual actually stated that he presumed something was being conducted based upon my approach and patterns. Fortunately, we continue to be friends and each of us has improved our critical thinking skills; however, there will be situations in which your outcome may not be so positive. When you begin to practice critical thinking, there is a possibility that you will receive some resistance from your circle, including family. They will immediately notice a change and possibly feel challenged, responding accordingly. There will be far less people that embrace your journey, but always remember that you make a difference just being an example.

Critical Thinking Processes and Self Evaluation

There are a number of processes or procedures that can be utilized to improve or enhance your critical thinking. According to The Miniature Guide to Critical Thinking Concepts and Tools, Foundation for Critical Thinking (Paul, Elder), well cultivated critical thinkers follow a similar pattern. A well cultivated critical thinker:

- thinks open-mindedly within alternative systems of thought, recognizing and assessing, as need be, their assumptions, implications, and practical consequences
- raises vital questions and problems, formulating them clearly and precisely
- gathers and assesses relevant information, utilizing abstract ideas to interpret it effectively
- reaches well-reasoned conclusions and solutions, while testing them against relevant criteria and standards
- communicates effectively with others in figuring out solutions to complex problems

Pursuing the path of critical thinking will require constant self-evaluation. In any endeavor of learning, you always want to be able to check your progress or possibly adjust your path of learning. Each person currently possesses a level of critical thinking skills even though we might be unaware of this fact. According to research conducted by the Foundation of Critical Thinking (Paul, Elder), there are six stages of critical thinking. Review the stages below and determine your position. This will give you an indication of your current level and the definition of the remaining stages. Keep in mind, there is no requirement that each person must reach the Master Thinker stage. You determine your individual growth. Take up the challenge and begin to take control of your thinking!

- *Stage One: The Unreflective Thinker* - The Unreflective thinkers are largely unaware of the determining role that thinking is playing in their lives and of the many ways that problems in thinking are causing problems in their lives. Unreflective thinkers lack the ability to explicitly assess their thinking and improve it.
- *Stage Two: The Challenged Thinker* - Thinkers move to the "challenged" stage when they become initially aware of the determining role that thinking is playing in their lives and of the act that problems in their thinking are causing them significant problems.
- *Stage Three: The Beginning Thinker* - Those who move to the beginning thinker stage are actively taking up the challenge to take explicit command of their thinking across multiple domains of their lives. Thinkers at this

stage recognize that they have basic problems in their thinking and make initial attempts to better understand how they can take charge and improve it. Based on this initial understanding, beginning thinkers begin to modify a part of their thinking but have limited insight into deeper levels of the trouble inherent in their thinking. Most importantly, they lack a systematic plan for improving their thinking; hence their efforts are hit and miss.

- *Stage Four: The Practicing Thinker* - Thinkers at this stage have a sense of the habits they need to develop to take charge of their thinking. They not only recognize that problems exist in their thinking, but they also recognize the need to attack these problems globally and systematically. Based on their sense of the need to practice regularly, they are actively analyzing their thinking in a number of domains. Since practicing thinkers are only beginning to approach the improvement of their thinking in a systematic way, they still have limited insight into deeper levels of thought, and thus into deeper levels of the problems embedded in thinking.
- *Stage Five: The Advanced Thinker* - Thinkers at this stage have now established good habits of thought which are "paying off." Based on the good habits, advanced thinkers not only actively analyze their thinking in

all the significant domains of their lives but also have significant insight into problems at deeper levels of thought. While advanced thinkers are able to think well across the important dimensions of their lives, they are not yet able to think at a consistently high level across all of these dimensions. Advanced thinkers have good general command over their egocentric nature. They continually strive to be fair-minded. Of course, they sometimes lapse into egocentrism and reason in a one-sided way.

- *Stage Six: The Master Thinker* - Master thinkers not only have systematically taken charge of their thinking but are also continually monitoring, revising, and re-thinking strategies for continual improvement of their thinking. They have deeply internalized the basic skills of thought so that critical thinking is, for them, both conscious and highly intuitive. They regularly raise their thinking to the level of conscious realization. Through extensive experience and practice in engaging in self-assessment, master thinkers are not only actively analyzing their thinking in all the significant domains of their lives but are also continually developing new insights into problems at deeper levels of thought. Master thinkers are deeply committed to fair-minded thinking and have a high level of control.

In addition to the previously listed methods, the Foundation of Critical Thinking has developed nine strategies (Paul, Elder) that can also be utilized to develop those skills. The strategies are basic in nature and require little effort to implement. Begin to test the referenced information to determine your comfort level within this topic.

Use "wasted" time

Address a problem a day

Internalize intellectual standards

Keep an intellectual journal

Reshape your character

Deal with your ego

Redefine the way you see things

Get in touch with your emotions

Analyze group influences on your life

Roadblocks of Critical Thinking

As with any type of personal growth, you will face resistance or roadblocks. Having the ability to recognize these types of distractions is crucial. During my research of this subject, I discovered a number of individuals that have revealed a number of critical thinking obstructions. Even from the list below, I immediately recognized a number of roadblocks that I have faced in my past and, unfortunately, continue to face daily. We must increase our sensitivity to roadblocks in our daily routines. We must be sensitive to our habits and be able to identify opportunities that allow us to master this process. According to the book The Thinker's Guide to the Art of Strategic Thinking: 25 Weeks to Better Thinking and Better Living (Paul, Elder), there are a number of actions that hinder critical thinking.

Jump to conclusions	Miss key ideas	Think narrowly
Lose track of their goal	Accept inaccurate information	Make poor decisions
Unrealistic	Focus on the trivial	Misuse words
Ignore relevant viewpoints	Unaware of our prejudices	Little insight into our own ignorance
Think egocentrically	Poor communicators	Think irrationally
Often make unjustified assumptions	Coming to unreasonable conclusions	Fail to think through implications

Do any of the listed roadblocks apply in your world? Honestly, I have been guilty of the majority of this list throughout my life, but as I made a conscious effort to self evaluate consistently, my list is gradually reducing. I challenge you to test a few of the critical thinking strategies, and I promise you that clarity will be your reward.

Be inquisitive, ask questions, fall in love with research, always evolve, demand this type of thinking from your inner circle and even expose your children to the art of critical thinking. Enjoy your journey!

Chapter Two

Hidden Beauty of a Woman

Self Discovery

"Gentlemen, what will it be?" asks the waitress.

Jeff responds, "I will have a half slab of your delicious barbecue ribs with extra sauce, a side of potato salad, baked beans and three extra slices of bread. Follow that up with a piece of peach cobbler, and I hope it tastes as good as my mother's cobbler. Oh, and start me off with a nice cold beer in a bottle."

"And you, sir?" asks the waitress.

Kevin responds, "Give me the fried catfish, collard greens, candied yams, macaroni and cheese and a large order of your homemade banana pudding for dessert, and I will also start with a cold beer."

"Great, I will be right out with your drinks." responds the waitress.

"Jeff, I cannot believe you have been married for ten years!" states Kevin.

"Yea, I can't believe how time flies," states Jeff. "It seems like yesterday that Sandra and I were walking down the aisle."

"How do you do it? How do you keep it fresh? How do you hold that passion for one woman for so many years?" asks Kevin.

"I keep it fresh by always searching for the hidden beauty in my wife." states Jeff.

"What the hell is that?" asks Kevin.

Jeff responds, "You see, this society is conditioned to focus only on the outer beauty of a woman. For instance, when you watch television or notice an ad in a magazine, all you will ever see are slim, beautiful women. The industry wants you to believe that this is the true essence of beauty for a woman. Women and men are inundated with these images, and it creates a false sense of self for many women. It also strips away a very important component of many women, the hidden beauty of a woman. What I mean by the hidden beauty is that there are so many internal characteristics. The exterior of a woman is just one component that defines "beauty." But there is so much more to women than just outer beauty. For instance, when I began to seek the hidden beauty of my wife, in addition to admiring her outer beauty, I discovered so many things about her that never even crossed my mind. At that point, I made a conscious decision to continue down that path. I have not only discovered so much about my wife, but this experience helped my wife discover things about herself. When you genuinely seek the best in someone and share the experiences, this just creates a stronger bond and appreciation for your relationship."

"What are some of the things that you look for?" asks Kevin.

"I look for the most important things in an individual. I look for a good heart. I look to see if she has compassion for others, including total strangers. I look to see if she constantly seeks to reach out to others that are less fortunate. I look to see if she genuinely believes in right and wrong. I look to see if she is seeking internal peace. I look to see if she is following her passion in life. I look to see if she is a loving mom and is committed to nurturing and caring for our children. I look to see if she is capable of handling the everyday burdens that she faces and able to intelligently address each issue without missing a beat. I look to see if she really loves me for who I am with all of my flaws. This is how I search for that beauty," Jeff passionately explained.

"Wow, that is beautiful. It never dawned on me that there are so many internal attributes involved in a woman. I've always focused on the outer beauty of a woman and have always fallen short in my relationships. I guess I still have a lot to learn about women," responds Kevin.

Jeff responds, "Well my friend, you will be fine. With anyone that you deal with, I suggest that the first thing that you do is to seek the best in that individual. It is a win-win for all. Adjust your thinking just a little and seek the hidden beauty in women. I promise you that you will not be disappointed. This discovery will be truly rewarding not only for you but for your partner. Enjoy the journey as I do," states Jeff with an enormous smile.

Even at my current stage in life, I am still amazed that many individuals lack the belief or confidence in themselves. Over many years of my life, I've always had a fascination for hearing success stories of people reaching their goals or having breakthroughs in their lives concerning their happiness. Unfortunately, at the same time, I have met many more individuals that are totally void of self confidence. Many people are totally disconnected from their inner attributes which make each and every person special in their individual way. Even though many people have mastered the art of great exterior presentation and the ability to mislead people into believing that all is well, internally they lack the essential tools that bring inner peace and a more fulfilling life.

For example, my wife is a prime example of an individual that did not recognize her inner beauty and full potential when we were first introduced. My wife's name is Victoria and we have been married for twenty beautiful and fulfilling years. I have been extremely fortunate to be a part of her life. She is a woman with inner and outer beauty; however, if you were to compare the Victoria of today to the Victoria of 1989 when we met, there would be little comparison. Fortunately, the present Victoria has thoroughly embraced life, committed herself to happiness/self improvement and faces life's challenges with confidence. She is a creative, confident, strong, and intuitive woman that is constantly seeking more out of life. She thrives on improving herself in a manner that fulfills her passion for life, and I support her 100% in her journey. I consistently encourage her to seek happiness and independence along with continuously searching for ways to complete herself. I do not require that she attempt to exist primarily to please her husband, and I can honestly say that my goal for her is to actively reach internally for her purpose in life. Even to the point of the two of us possibly parting ways. I have always stated that with or without me, I wish and encourage that her thirst for life, her growth and her way of thinking continue without interruption. I would want her to continue her pursuit of happiness within her life. Business as usual.

Now let's take some time to examine Ms. Victoria of 1989. When we met, she was a beautiful young lady at the beginning her career at a prestigious university. In just a few years out of college, she purchased her first home, a new automobile and launched a small business creating gift baskets. I was impressed. She also participated as a model in a number of local fashion events. She seemed to be a happy individual on her path to doing great things. The first time that we met, she informed me that there was someone in her life; however, my intention was to determine the seriousness of their relationship. She provided little information and minimal interest so I handed her my business card and asked her to call me if she wanted to meet for a drink. She kindly accepted the business card and we parted ways.

Approximately two months later, I received a phone call from Victoria. We talked for a few moments and I invited her out for a movie. She accepted, and we began to meet on occasion to talk. When we would meet, we would talk for long periods of time, and there was no subject off limits. Even though she seemed to be a happy individual taking advantage of what life had to offer, I began to notice that there was something below the surface of this beautiful rose that didn't coincide with her exterior presentation. I began to notice an uneasy demeanor that would overtake her periodically suggesting that there was unease in her life. When I eventually began to ask questions about her life and her current relationship, I quickly realized that she was eager to talk about her situation which turned out to be unfortunate and dysfunctional. At that point, I began to ask tough questions concerning her current situation and

I remember to this day my first question concerning her relationship. The question was simply: "Are you happy?" Her reaction was of pain and relief. It was if she had been harboring the pain waiting for someone to provide an opportunity to discuss her situation. She needed someone to talk to and as she explained, she had reached a tipping point. She was more than willing to share her situation.

With her feeling more comfortable with me, I chose to probe even more about her boyfriend. She informed me that her boyfriend was possessive and verbally abusive, and she believed that physical abuse was inevitable. She was afraid of this man and regretted the day she allowed him to share her home. Eventually experiencing physical abuse from him, she asked him to move, but he refused. While unwilling to conform to her request, one particular evening he actually displayed a firearm threatening to commit suicide if she tried to have him removed from her home. She immediately assumed that he would kill her first. Over time, this man forced her into isolation by deliberately removing her ties with her friends and family in order to gain more control. She reached a point in which she chose to leave her home only for work. She felt totally helpless and was fearful of this man. I immediately understood her situation because I was aware of a number of scenarios where women were experiencing this type of entrapment. I really wanted to help. It was just the right thing to do, so I simply asked her "How can I help?" She softly responded, "I just want him out of my house!" and welcomed my assistance.

Before I continue with Victoria's story, let me give you a brief description of her ex-boyfriend. This man actually moved into her home and refused to offer any assistance with the mortgage payment or utilities. He contributed nothing toward household needs, such as groceries or maintenance. He constantly purchased a large amount of clothes and shoes, in addition to owning both a BMW and a Mercedes convertible. To top it off, he was gainfully employed as an accountant. What a guy!

Back to Victoria's story. From my perspective at that time, her request was quite simple and I responded with my patented response, "No problem!" I felt that this would be a no brainer. My impulse solution was simple. Catch his ass in a remote location with one or two of my boys and "have a chat." Piece of cake. But after carefully assessing the situation, this type of reaction had the potential to create negative consequences for a number of individuals involved. There could be a possible physical retaliation toward Victoria and/or myself or possibly a legal situation. After returning home that evening, I began to ask myself how my parents would approach this type of situation.

Reflecting on their teachings, their first action would be to take the emotion out of the problem and address the problem in a logical manner, which includes a well thought out plan. A much more logical starting point than my first thought.

First plan of attack, I began to work closely with Victoria to gather intel on this individual. I documented his full name, auto tag numbers, place of employment and a list of venues that he frequently visited. I made copies of the information and gave a copy to a friend who was a city police officer. He also provided a wealth of information in reference to addressing the problem.

While I was gathering information on this guy, I discovered that he was gathering information concerning me, which was no surprise. One evening after returning from dinner with Victoria, we retreated to my apartment to relax and provide Victoria with a little quiet time away from her home. While watching a movie, I receive a phone call. It was actually Victoria's boyfriend calling my home! At that moment, I was totally involved in this situation.

My first reaction was to ask him politely not to call my home. He then went into this ranting and cursing mode telling me that he was going to "kick my ass" and ordering me to meet him in my parking lot. He was actually sitting outside of my apartment. "Oh really?" I responded. This man is in the parking lot of my home! I needed to address this issue immediately. I informed Victoria and my roommate of the situation and then called my friend who was the police officer. It is always better to be cautious in those types of situations. I did not want to be a statistic over some emotional situation. Victoria insisted that she should meet him outside and talk with him; however, I disagreed with her recommendation, fearing for her safety, so I made a decision to meet this guy since he insisted on invading my space. As I headed for the door, Victoria stopped me to remind me that he owned a firearm, which I anticipated. As a strategic ploy, I asked my roommate to stand on our balcony, which provided a view of the parking lot. I walked out of the front door and began to walk down the flight of stairs. My apartment was located on the third floor, and he actually had a view of each flight of stairs. When I reached the second flight of stairs, I heard the sound of his engine, but his car did not move. By the time that I approached the last flight of stairs, he immediately placed the car in reverse and quickly departed from the apartment complex. Honestly, I was truly relieved that he decided to leave because those types of incidents are extremely unpredictable and many times the outcome is negative for both parties. It is never good to place yourself in a dangerous situation.

After this point, it was time to address this issue with Victoria. First thing was to sit with her and discuss her true position on this matter. I needed to determine if she truly wanted this guy out of her life or if there were other motives. She needed to convince me as if she was facing life in prison and I had the final vote for conviction. I was not going to put forth any more effort toward her dilemma if she was still in love with this man or there was a possibility of reconciliation. After explaining my position and asking her about this matter, her response was quite forceful. She glared into my eyes and stated, "I do not love him and I want him out of my life! He is only in my life at this time because he will not leave my home and I am afraid of him!" Damn! She could have a career as an actress on a soap opera. I was truly convinced of her intentions and it had nothing to do with the fact that I wanted a taste of her cookies. In any event, I recommended that she stay at my apartment that evening just for safety concerns. The next morning, I met with my friend on the police force to receive some feedback concerning the previous night's activities. Keeping law enforcement informed was important.

After that incident, I had to quickly develop a plan, a carefully crafted plan utilizing my standard process for dealing with problems: PROBLEM, SOLUTION, ACTION. First thing is to carefully define and evaluate your problem.

Second, gather data to develop a well thought out solution/plan to address your problem. And third, strategically implement your plan reaching your primary goal(s). To maximize the impact of such a process, it was time to reach out to my mentor network.

The majority of my life, I have been fortunate to have access to a number of mentors. Beginning with my parents and family/neighborhood elders spanning to career/ life mentors, I have always depended upon council from experienced individuals. As a child, I was truly blessed with an infrastructure that provided a wealth of nurturing, protection and learning. As an adult, in addition to my family, I have included resources that provide career/life expertise in various industries such as financial, business, technology, etc.

Concerning my current crisis, I carefully selected a mentor that would understand my situation and would take offense as if he/she were facing the problem. I made my choice and called to schedule a time to meet. This particular gentleman was an extremely intelligent engineer and a graduate of the top engineering university in the world. I highly respected this man and, at one point in my career, I was fortunate to have him as my supervisor. Having the opportunity to sit with this man was truly priceless. We decided to meet during one of our standard monthly sessions. We met at least once a month on Saturday mornings just to visit and brainstorm on different business ideas. There was a standard routine with each of my mentors. Keeping to our standard session routine, I arrived at his home at 7:00 a.m. sharp, and his lovely wife had breakfast prepared for the three of us served on their deck. Alan's morning task was to prepare the Bloody Marys. Their deck spanned the length of their home and was surrounded by a two-tiered water feature cascading into a large coy pond. It was a very relaxing environment. After we finished breakfast, his wife left for an appointment, leaving us to our own devices. Alan and I refreshed our morning libations and began our session.

After explaining my situation, he asked three direct questions: "Is she OK?", "Is this young lady serious about separating from this man?" and "Are you certain that you want to get involved?" I answered yes to each question. He responded "Well, let's move on." He then asked me to help him understand our overall goal. I explained that Victoria's overall goal was to remove this man from her home and my goal was to provide any assistance and a level of security. He carefully listened and we continued to discuss the matter at hand for approximately an hour. After our discussion, Alan made a comment that never crossed my mind in my entire life. "If you ever want to get someone to respond to a situation or a request, initiate an event that will negatively affect their way of life." The comment was not entirely clear at that moment, and I asked him to restate and explain. He restated his comment and began to explain his theory. An individual's livelihood/survival is one of the most important components in their life. If their way of life is somewhat threatened, you will get their undivided attention. In other words, fuck with their money and you will definitely get their undivided attention.

He began to ask a number of questions in order to get me to think through the situation. As he began to gather data from my responses, I noticed a pattern in his questioning. His strategy was quite simple: 1) Identify a situation that could be leveraged to threaten the boyfriend's lifestyle. 2) How does he generate his income? To address the first task, I talked with Victoria about the abusive behavior. Apparently, this guy also threatened her with bodily harm at her place of employment. In addition to the abuse, he vandalized her vehicle on the property of her employer. What an idiot!

I obtained his employer information some time before our meeting. As we were both aware, my mentor began to explain that corporations and government employers have a zero tolerance concerning verbal and physical abuse, as well as sexual harassment, in the workplace. These types of actions can lead to a person's termination. So we decided to indiscreetly share his abusive behavior with his employer. My question was, *How would we get the information to his workplace?* With a phone call to his supervisor? Possibly utilize the press? In a letter form? What would be the best vehicle in this matter? Alan responded that a well drafted letter would handle the problem; however, the impact of the letter is measured by the delivery method. I was clearly confused at this point, but he continued to explain. If the letter is addressed to his superior using direct mail, there is a possibility that he has a great relationship with his boss and his boss may protect his employee and bury the letter so that no one is informed of this man's actions. We did not want to take a chance on that scenario. Alan suggested the following: Fax the letter to his employer without a cover letter. In most cases, someone within the office other than his supervisor will notice the fax and read the content in order to determine the receiver. Once this is done, office politics begins and there is a likely chance that this information will reach a number of individuals in the company. Not a bad idea! After refreshing our Bloody Marys, we crafted a one page letter detailing each harassment incident. The final letter was addressed to his employer and signed by me with Victoria being unaware of my actions. The next morning, I conveniently faxed the letter to his job.

The following day, Victoria received her first response. This guy was extremely upset and constantly calling my apartment leaving a number of inappropriate and threatening messages. I assumed the letter reached the appropriate parties and the outcome was exactly what we were expecting. Even better, on the following Saturday morning, he actually packed his belongings and moved out of Victoria's home. The calls to Victoria's place of employment ceased, the calls to her home stopped, and the calls to my home stopped. The recommended process was highly effective. To this day, I clearly remember Alan's sound feedback in reference to how people protect their way of life. People will do what needs to be done to protect there territory.

At that point, Victoria and I had been dating close to four months. There was no commitment between us. We were just dating and basically having a good time. With that in mind, I expressed to her that I did not expect a commitment from her based upon assisting with her dilemma, but I expressed that I was interested in continuing our friendship. My participation was based solely upon the principles instilled in me by my parents. I recognized that she had experienced a lot over the last two years and she might want to be alone for awhile. I was truly content if this were to be her position. Well, fortunate for me, she wanted to continue dating, and she became my wife.

As I stated earlier in this chapter, from that point forward, I made a conscious effort to always tell her that she was a strong, intuitive, beautiful and creative woman that should constantly seek more out of life which will provide her pleasure, peace and happiness. Today, she thrives on bettering herself in a manner that fulfills her passion in life. In return, she provides fulfillment for me as her husband.

Unfortunately, there are many women who face this type of circumstance where a man purposely attacks their inner strength in order to gain control. When a person is losing their inner strength, unfortunately, many begin to seek comfort in their exterior beauty, gradually ignoring their inner beauty. They begin to mask their unhappiness and seek approval from entities outside of themselves. Many women refuse to believe that they are beautiful individuals who possess all of the attributes required to achieve total belief in oneself. For some reason, this is becoming more and more of an issue in our world today. I am here to tell you that it has been proven that there is no make-up product, clothing line, or cosmetic surgery procedure available today that will substitute for inner beauty and self confidence. You must possess the capacity to believe in you and continue to search for inner peace and confidence.

One of the methods of building confidence is to investigate the history and current state of women. When you identify and acknowledge the considerable number of accomplishments and milestones that women achieved throughout the course of history, your results can be established as a foundation for your journey. Women are the beginning and, for centuries, have made great strides and continue to excel at alarming rates. Let's take a moment to examine a few facts concerning the impact of you, your daughter, mother, grandmother, friend, niece, and neighbor. Let's begin with a few quotes concerning the strength and excellence of women and the pursuit of self-awareness:

"Educate a Woman, You Educate a Nation!" (Mlambo-Ngcuka)

"The whole point of being alive is to evolve into the complete person you were intended to be." (Winfrey)

"Tomorrows' woman will not be guided by how the world judges her. She will live her life on her terms based upon self-acceptance." (Unknown)

Did you happen to notice the power and energy in the above statements? Are you beginning to get my point?

- As a woman, you are complete as you are today. You currently possess the tools within to experience fulfillment and happiness in your life.
- Women are the bearers and nurturers of all humans. A woman's womb is noted as the central energy source and gateway for all mankind. (Queen Afua)

- Scholars have proven that there were a large number of matriarchal or non-patriarchal societies throughout human history. Many believe that matriarchy is the foundation of civilization.
- For those comfortable with exploring different belief systems, there is a belief that we are in an Aquarian Age or Age of Aquarius. This is considered the age of enlightenment and self-awareness. (Perrone)
- In the 2008 school year, 57 percent of all the bachelor's degrees and 61 percent of all the master's degrees were earned by women. (The Condition of Education)
- Four out of the eight Ivy League universities--Harvard, Brown, Penn and Princeton--have female presidents.
- The buying power of U.S. women is estimated at $7 trillion. Women are expected to control more than $22 trillion by 2012. (Women's Statistics)
- More than 52% of the US workforce is women. Women business owners employ more than 12 million Americans and contribute $3.6 trillion to the national economy.
- Over 70% of new businesses are started by women.
- Women account for 52% of internet users.
- Women are responsible for 83% of consumer based purchases including home furnishings (94%), vacations (92%), homes (91%), healthcare (80%), food (93%), bank accounts (89%).

- International Women's Day – IWD is a global day celebrating the economic, political and social achievements of women, past, present and future.

Damn, I am loving this! The information above is just a glimpse of your accomplishments. There is an abundance of additional information that clearly justifies your value and the importance of your presence. The trick is that you must exert a conscious effort to discover this content.

You must also be aware that there are consequences if you choose not to know thyself. Many studies have indicated that not knowing yourself can possibly lead to life choices that are inconsistent with your true journey. Psychologist Helene Brenner, Ph.D., author of I Know I'm In There Somewhere, states, "It is every woman's birthright to live from her true self. Yet instead, women live their lives standing outside themselves, always ready to judge their feelings, their thoughts and their bodies from an external standard and find themselves wanting." Unfortunately, a number of industries have recognized this condition among women and have chosen to capitalize financially by creating an industry that drives the importance of outer beauty while totally disregarding the importance of your inner strength. I happen to be speaking of the cosmetic industry.

Please understand that I am not declaring war against the beauty/cosmetic industry. The beauty industry has produced a number of great products and solutions that truly enhance the exterior beauty of a woman. Daily, I am fortunate to witness a number of beautiful women (such as my wife) that have stunning appearances based partly upon beauty products. We, however, must also remember to place just as much effort in the development of our inner beauty. Understanding that cosmetic products and beauty solutions are an integral part of many lives, it is in our best interest to at least be aware of the industry facts.

Cosmetic/Beauty Industry and Its Impact on Women

Today, we are constantly reminded of the importance of outer beauty. People are obsessed with facial features, weight, body shapes, etc. From a shot of Botox, breast implants, or layers of make-up to buttocks augmentation, we are obsessed with outer improvement. There are even companies creating cosmetics for girls as young as eight years of age, and teenagers are receiving surgery enhancements by the age 19. Unfortunately, the importance of outer beauty has taken a front seat in many women's' lives and is beginning to affect our children.

How much are we spending to retain our youth? What is the revenue generated by the beauty industry? According to a market research report, Cosmetic Surgery Markets: Products and Services by ReportLinker.com, a forecast of the global market for cosmetic surgery services will reach $40 billion by the year 2013, up from $31.7 billion in 2008. The global market for cosmetic products is estimated to reach $7 billion in 2013, up from $4.4 billion in 2008. In the U.S. in 2007, the largest demographic group for individuals who experienced a cosmetic surgery procedure was individuals between the ages of 40 and 54, a total of 5.5 million procedures. The second largest group was individuals 55 and older, which totaled 3.1 million procedures. According to a study by American Society of Plastic Surgeons (Britt), more than 55 million cosmetic surgery procedures will be performed worldwide in 2015. This is incredible! Oh, and it continues...

According to the American Society of Plastic Surgeons Report of the 2010 Plastic Surgery Statistics, the top five cosmetic surgical procedures performed in the U.S. included breast augmentation (296,203), eyelid surgery (208,764), liposuction (203,106), nose reshaping (252,261), and tummy tuck (116,352) in 2010. The overall number of cosmetic surgical procedures in the U.S. totaled 1,555,614. In addition, the top five minimally-invasive cosmetic procedures included botox (5,379,360), chemical peel (1,144,865), laser hair removal (937,602), microdermabrasion (824,706), and hyaluronic acid (1,201,368) in 2010. Cosmetic procedures in the U.S. in 2010 totaled 13,117,063.

Again, I am not against the beauty industry. I am simply informing the customers of their personal impact on this industry. In addition to the revenue numbers, there are a number of researchers who have expressed intriguing views concerning the overall purpose of the beauty industry. Nancy Etcoff, author of Survival of the Prettiest and a supporter of the beauty industry, believes that this industry is necessary for the perpetuation of the human race. Ms. Etcoff argues that beauty improvements present a person's appearance as fertile and healthy to attract a mate. Offering an opposing view, Naomi Wolf, author of The Beauty Myth – How Images of Beauty are Used Against Women, argues that women in the Western culture face pressure to conform to an idealized concept of female beauty. These are quite interesting theories; however, the development of your inner beauty is far more important than any exterior solution.

Attributes of Inner Beauty

One of the first steps required in enhancing or simply improving your inner beauty is to identify a number of key attributes of inner beauty. Once you become aware of a number of core attributes, you can begin to evaluate and integrate into your daily routine. One of the methods that I use to ingrain these types of attributes into my brain is by association. In every situation where I am interacting with individuals, I try to associate someone's actions or demeanor with one or more of the attributes listed below. For example, one of my many self-induced therapy sessions consists of enjoying a nice cigar along with friends. During this time, I observe a number of individuals with the intention of connecting an inner beauty attribute. If I hear someone expressing their love for their wife, I associate that action with love. When a gentleman is adamantly defending an individual asking to "give him a chance," I associate that action with compassion. This is just one of a number of methods that I use to ingrain this type of behavior. A partial list is below…

- Truth – The quality of being true; sincerity, genuineness, honesty.
- Good Character – The definition of character is moral or ethical quality. According to The Josephson Institute of Ethics, there are Six Pillars of Character: trustworthiness, respect, responsibility, fairness, caring, and citizenship.
- Inner Peace – Inner peace can be characterized as an individual's sense of self, being spiritually and mentally at peace, state of enlightenment or consciousness developed by meditation, prayer or other forms of training.
- Love – One act of love is to allow individuals to choose to believe in their interpretation of most things. When

Confucius, a Chinese thinker and social philosopher, was asked "What is love?", he responded, "Love is to conquer self and turn to courtesy. Could we conquer self and turn to courtesy for but one day, all mankind would turn to love." Love is slow to speak. Love is to love mankind.

- Joy – The passion or emotion excited by the acquisition or expectation of good; pleasurable feeling or emotions caused by success or good fortune; gladness, exhilaration of spirits.
- Purity – Purity is mainly defined as demonstrating authentic or genuine truth; the quality or condition of being pure.
- Compassion – Sympathetic consciousness of others' distress together with a desire to alleviate; wanting others to be free from suffering whether another is a close friend or enemy; qualities of sharing, readiness to give comfort, sympathy, concern, caring (Buddhism). Compassion views without judgment of the other. Compassion does not condemn and is capable of kindness.
- Integrity – Firm adherence to ethical and moral values; moral soundness, honesty, freedom from corrupting influence or motive; consistency of actions, methods, values, methods, measures, principles, and outcome.

- Patience – The quality of being patient, as the bearing of provocation, annoyance, misfortune, or pain, without complaint, loss of temper or irritation; good human characteristic or a positive psychological attitude, by virtue of which we refrain from doing that which is not good.
- Knowledge – The acquisition of perception, learning, communication, association and reasoning; confident understanding of a subject with the ability to use it for a specific purpose; that which is gained and preserved by knowing, enlightenment, learning, and/or scholarship.
- Healthy Living – State of complete physical, mental, and social well-being (Health); steps, actions and strategies one puts in place to achieve optimum health; taking responsibility and making smart health choices for today and for the future; eating right, getting physically fit, emotional wellness, spiritual wellness and prevention.
- Great Smile – An excellent way to improve your health, attractiveness and stress level; smiling can change your mood, relieve stress, boost your immune system, and is contagious according to Elizabeth Scott, M.S. Smiling lowers your blood pressure, makes you look younger, projects confidence and success, helps you stay positive, and inspires others.

- Sense of Humor/Laughter – Humor inspires hope, connects you to others, and keeps you grounded, focused, and alert. Humor helps you keep a positive, optimistic outlook through difficult situations, disappointments, and misfortune. Humor increases intimacy and happiness. Humor strengthens your immune system, boosts your energy, and decreases pain and stress. Laughter relaxes your body, and protects the heart by increasing blood flow. Laughter improves your mood, adds joy to life, strengthens relationships, and helps defuse conflict. (Smith)
- Personal Confidence – Defined as realistic confidence in oneself or one's own abilities; freedom from doubt; belief in yourself and your abilities; having optimism, assertiveness, enthusiasm, independence, pride.
- Self Esteem – Overall evaluation or appraisal of your own worth; pride in yourself. Self esteem is the opinion you have of yourself; based upon how a person perceives his/her value as a person with regard to work, status, achievements, purpose in life, your perceived place in the social order, strengths and weaknesses, how you relate to others and your ability to stand on your own feet. (Sihera)

Self Evaluation of Your Inner Beauty

As you begin to infuse inner beauty attributes into your thinking, we want to take some time to reflect on our individual level of inner beauty. Take a moment for self evaluation. Take a moment to take an honest look at yourself. This will be fun! The road to discovery is a journey, and the journey requires patience, discipline and the burning desire to reach your goal. In addition to your individual work, please realize that you are not alone on your mission. There are a number of individuals and resources available to provide assistance. Seek individuals that are on a similar path to keep you motivated for your inner beauty workout as you do with your physical workout such as keeping a journal of your progress. Results happen over a period of time, so a consistent routine is required. Below is information that can be viewed as either a launching point or merely supplemental information for your inner beauty workout.

- Self Acceptance – Acknowledge that you deserve the best for your life; being happy with who you are at this very moment; being able to accept all things about ourselves; evaluate and then fully accept ourselves; individual's satisfaction or happiness with self; self understanding.

- Self Reflection – The capacity of an individual to learn more about their individual fundamental purpose and nature; the ability to look in the mirror and perceive ourselves; the ability to be responsible within one's own life. The art of self reflection creates empowerment for an individual; we need to understand ourselves and eventually advance to understanding the fundamental nature of our existence.
- Self Motivation – Self motivation is the ability to satisfy a goal, expectation or desire without the influence of others; the ability to motivate yourself, to find a reason and strength to do something, without the need of being; development of perseverance and mental attitude.
- Self Awareness – Self awareness begins with the fundamental understanding of your existence, awareness of one's own individuality; Who am I? What are my overall strengths, weaknesses, qualities? What are my values? What defines my personality? What are my habits? What is the purpose of knowing thyself? Where do we begin? Recognize the need to know thyself. In everyday tasks, become aware of what you do each day and evaluate why you do these things.
- Have a great imagination, dream – A strongly desired goal or purpose. An aspiration.

- Seek out, observe and surround yourself with people of positive inner strength – Position yourself to meet people that are on similar paths; locate and visit venues that embrace positive thought and thinking.
- Enjoy the Journey – View life as an interesting journey; begin to recognize all things around you and appreciate the existence of those things.
- Sever ties with negative individuals in your life (one of my favorites) – It is your responsibility to protect your positive energy; you must learn to evaluate your circle of friends and family and then eliminate relationships which hinder your growth. Individuals who harbor negative energy will prey on individuals with positive energy; you must be familiar with the signs to recognize these types of individuals. For example, people that are always complaining, people that are constantly blaming others for their situation, or individuals that are always talking about other individuals are prime examples of negative people. To begin the cleansing process, there are a number of methods that you can apply. First, if it is an individual that you can do without in your life, my opinion is just to sever ties permanently - no communication, no interaction, no assistance. If it is someone that is important in your life, you can begin by simply staying positive and offering

positive comments when you are in their presence or just stay silent when they are spreading their negative energy. One of my favorite strategies is to actually relate an incident to a higher sign or signal. I strongly believe that when an individual successfully penetrates my energy skin, it is a sign from a higher power informing me that it is time to remove the source. My time with this individual is complete and I received my instructions to continue my journey in another space. I must thank them for their time and forge ahead.

- Trust your intuition, Trust your instincts, Trust your gut – According to TimeForChange.org, intuition is receiving input and ideas without knowing exactly how and where you got them or instinctive and unconscious knowing without deduction or reasoning. Many times, intuition is categorized as an inner voice, spiritual voice, gut feeling, sixth sense. As Dr. Robin Smith urged on the Oprah Show, trust your gut!
- Embrace Change – Living in a world without borders, there are a number of cultures and belief systems in place today. Each one of us has a belief system, most likely based upon our family and cultural backgrounds. It is extremely important and beneficial however to begin or continue to examine different ways of thinking. Before the internet and the immersion of technology,

information was not readily available. Now we have access to information which can provide a wealth of content concerning other cultures and beliefs. We have the ability to study other belief systems even in the comfort of our homes.

- Encourage other women and young girls to develop inner beauty – Be an advocate for positive thinking. Be an example to women and girls of all ages. Conduct a seminar in your community. Always exert a positive smile and offer compliments and encouragement to others.
- Spend some personal/quiet time alone doing something that you enjoy or makes you happy – Enough said. This might seem like a tough one, but it's important to make it happen!
- Meditation/Prayer – Meditation is an ancient process or method of connecting the mind and body in order to achieve a specific goal. Meditation is used to reduce stress and is a central component within religion and outside religion. There are a number of types of meditation techniques such as breath watching, walking meditation, or transcendental meditation.
- Yoga – Originated in India, Yoga is an ancient system of physical exercises, breathing practices, postures and meditation which provide a union between the mind,

body and spirit. The word Yoga is derived from the Sanskrit word, yukti, which means union, connect, join or balance and is utilized to achieve inner happiness, self-enlightenment and self-realization.

- Take time to play, foster your inner child – Anyone open for sky diving? Set no limits!
- Become a role model – Make the time for someone in your life. No agenda required, just your time and attention.

This is just a brief list of tasks that you can implement into your daily routine. Always remember that we are all connected and with this understanding, you will develop a broader outlook on life that expands our individual belief system.

Intrapersonal Intelligence

While researching the content for this book, I discovered a gentleman who developed the theory of Multiple Intelligences. Dr. Howard Gardner, professor of Education at Harvard University, stresses the importance of recognizing and nurturing all of the human intelligences and all of the combinations of intelligences. How does the theory of Multiple Intelligences relate to inner beauty? In his research, Dr. Gardner identifies eight intelligences, one of which is an integral component of inner beauty.

Developed in 1983, Dr. Gardner's theory proposes that children and adults possess eight different intelligences that enable a broader range of learning. His theory is primarily geared toward the primary/secondary education system, explaining how children are viewed in regards to their individual intelligence but is equally applicable to adults. Dr. Gardner believes that we should place equal attention on individuals who demonstrate gifts in various intelligences: artists, architects, musicians, designers, therapists, entrepreneurs, naturalists and others who enrich the world in which we live.

How does intrapersonal intelligence relate to inner beauty? Individuals that have high intrapersonal intelligence are more likely to be independent, self-confident and self-motivated (Teele). Let's review the definition. Intrapersonal Intelligence is defined as having self awareness components, such as the capacity to self-reflect; understanding of yourself; knowing who you are, what you can do, and what you want to do; knowing how you react to things, which things to avoid, and which things to gravitate toward. This particular knowledge is based upon a profoundly focused understanding of self, your strengths, weaknesses, and insecurities. According to Frames of Mind: The Theory of Multiple Intelligences by Dr. Gardner, the core capacity of intrapersonal intelligence is the access to your individual range of feelings or emotions. Intrapersonal intelligence is clearly defined as "the capacity instantly to effect discriminations among these feelings and, eventually, to label them, to enmesh them in symbolic codes, to draw upon them as a means of understanding and guiding one's behavior" or the ability to detect and to symbolize complex and highly differentiated sets of feelings.

Dr. Gardner represents a number of scholars that have committed to simply discovering and informing you of different types of methodologies that can truly enhance your understanding of self or inner beauty. Continue your growth and share your experiences and energy with others.

Chapter Three

A Brief History of Marriage

Is Marriage for You?

"Oh sweetheart, you are going to be such a beautiful bride," states mom as she watches her daughter try on her wedding gown during her fitting. "I have been waiting for this day for many years."

"Ladies, can I get you anything?" asks the attendant of the bridal shop.

"Yes, my dear, bring us a bottle of your best champagne," responds mom.

"May I recommend something to snack on such as Beluga caviar with Greek olives, an assortment of fine cheeses and fresh strawberries?" offers the attendant.

"Yes, that would be wonderful," responds mom. Mom then turns to her daughter and continues their conversation, "Kelly,

John is a wonderful man. He loves you dearly, and the two of you are going to have a great family. You are a lucky lady. I can't wait to spoil my grandchildren, especially if we have a girl or maybe twins. I can envision many hours of shopping."

Glazing into the mirror, Kelly responds, "Now mom, let's not rush things. John and I have decided to take the first few years to get to know each other and spend some quality time together before we commit to the responsibilities of parenthood. That issue will not be something that we address immediately, and sometimes I wonder if I really want children."

"But sweetheart, children are such a joy, and I don't want you to miss one moment of that opportunity. When your father and I married, you were born one year later."

"Yes I understand, mom, but times have changed. John and I have our careers that we both enjoy and are not willing to give up at this time."

"Well, as long as you are happy with your marriage, I guess that is a good start. What's the problem, dear?" asks mom. "You can talk to me."

"Mom, I don't know if I want to go through with this," says Kelly.

"Go through with what?" mom asks sharply, "What are you saying, dear?"

The daughter responds, "I am unsure about my decision to get married. I am beginning to doubt the institution of marriage.

For instance, take the divorce rate. The divorce rate is over fifty percent. Fifty percent, mom! And in addition to the divorce rate, I honestly can't tell you if I want to be with the same person for my entire life. I enjoy my career and it is unfair to me and Mike if I cannot give my all. And as I stated earlier, I might not want to have children. There are many other reasons why I feel this way and I feel bad that I allowed this process to get this far along without talking to you, dad and Mike. At this moment, I really have concerns about the institution of marriage."

"Sweetheart, I had no idea of your feelings. Don't worry. You are just experiencing pre-marital jitters. By this time tomorrow morning, all of your doubts will be a thing of the past. Trust me," states mom. "I was nervous when I married your father, but look at our lives. We have been married for thirty years and we are fine. Now we've had some tough times, but we made it and have a great life. We have a beautiful daughter, a nice home in a nice community and many friends that love us. Marriage has been great for us," states mom.

"I understand, mom, and I'm totally grateful for you and dad's commitment to each other and to me. But it is now a different era. In your era, marriage was the thing to do. For instance, you and dad were married at twenty years old, which means that you really didn't know each other. At that time, women were placed in a certain role of homemaker and men were the bread winners. I have to trust my intuition, and I am willing to face

the consequences from my decision. Mom, I love you and dad and this is something that I must do for my happiness. Please try to understand and wish me well. I need you to understand my position," states daughter.

"This is a lot to digest at the last minute. Please, dear, just give it some time. This will pass. You marry that man and all will work out," responds mom.

"Mom, this wedding is not going to happen! I must talk to Mike immediately. Please don't be disappointed in me. I need you and dad at this moment more than any other time. I love you both very much and thank you for being there," states daughter with a smile.

"OK, sweetheart. Follow your heart and it will all work out fine. Your father and I love you very much," explains mom with a smile.

The institution of marriage is a cornerstone of many cultures and has been in existence since the earliest known civilizations. For thousands of years, marriage has been a part of the foundation of human society and, with the evolution of culture, history, religion and politics, the concept of marriage has taken on many forms and continues to transform. There have been a number of marital traditions and customs established in accordance with the specific periods in history. For instance, if we take a look at the early part of history, you will find that for thousands of years, marriage was primarily a civil transaction or business transaction between families of the bride and groom. Customs such as a dowry, which is property or valuables provided by a bride's family given to the groom's family, was the focal point of the process and unfortunately coupled with minimal rights for the bride and the requirement to be subservient to groom. The concept of love was rarely a part of the marriage process. In Ancient Greece, marriage was a tool to form a political alliance between noble families. Under Roman law, the bride ceased to be a member of her family and control was passed completely to her husband. Marriage in the traditional Chinese society was arranged by families. Some situations allowed multiple wives; some were arranged marriages based upon financial commitments. Some were even based upon same sex. Today, the institution is based upon love opposed to ownership or alliances, and each person has the opportunity and right to select their mate and become intimately connected.

Over the past several generations, cultural shifts have prompted a number of questions about the institution of marriage. Where do we go from this point? What does the future hold for this institution? Will the current system of love continue, or is it failing? Will marriage even exist in a thousand years? Unfortunately, I do not possess the means to predict the future; however, I can examine past and present data which can provide possible insight of a marriage roadmap. I must admit that the current data does not paint a rosy picture. This is the reason for my curiosity of the subject of marriage. Please understand that I am not against the institution of marriage. Quite the opposite! I am a supporter of marriage and have been quite fortunate to witness a number of successful marriages in my lifetime. My wife and I have been happily married for twenty years and my parents are approaching sixty-five years of marital bliss. I must admit, my siblings and I are fortunate to have two loving parents who dedicated their lives to our well-being. Please allow me to share my family's story.

My mother and father have been married for more than 60 years and raised nine children (four girls and five boys); six were adopted (myself included), in addition to a number of foster children that were a part of our lives throughout our childhood years. This couple is truly special. Speaking for the adopted siblings, we are truly grateful to our parents for their dedication and commitment to raising us as if we were their biological children.

As men, my brothers and I are truly appreciative of our father. My father is the epitome of a man: father, mentor, provider, role model, and even little league baseball and flag football coach when we were children. He has always been committed to the wellbeing of his children.

Of course, my mother is the quintessential queen bee of the family. Overseer, nurturer, provider of unconditional love, spiritual leader and we must not forget, disciplinarian. "Spare the rod, spoil the child" was the motto in our home. Actually I believe that the discipline aspect was their form of entertainment. Our mother is one special person. I am the fourth oldest child of the family and the first son, I was fortunate to be given my father's name which has been a sense of pride for me throughout my life. I have three older sisters, all biological children of my parents. I was the first child to be adopted. I was six weeks old and my younger siblings were adopted at different intervals throughout my life. To this day, I love my family dearly and always enjoy the opportunity to share my family experience. Because of my good fortune, I am truly a supporter of the institution of marriage.

Still, it is my humble opinion that the current institution is failing and requires an overhaul. Many people that I talked with adamantly place the blame on the individuals claiming the institution itself has no part in the results. Of course, we understand that the parties are partly responsible, but you cannot totally disregard the composition of the institution. The institution is not exempt from evaluation. For example, if you are an owner of a company which is losing over fifty percent of its revenue based upon a specific strategy or framework, your first point of action would be to 1) review your people and 2) review your corporate strategy/processes. It would not be a wise decision to just place the fault on your team and ignore the existing strategy. This is not a good practice. This is where we are concerning the institution of marriage. Fortunately for us, there are a number of dedicated individuals and organizations that are conducting various studies focusing on the institution of marriage in order to discover possible data that will address our current system.

Over the years, I passively monitored the overall rates of marriage in today's society because of the large failure or divorce rate within our society. Why is the failure rate at an all time high? Is the institution of marriage becoming obsolete? And the question that no one is eager to address: Is there a need for marriage in our future? What about the wedding ceremony? We have systematically created an entire industry geared toward the wedding ceremony. The cost alone of a wedding can place a young couple in thousands of dollars of debt going into their marriage. Unfortunately, I have met couples whose ceremony lasted longer than their marriage itself. What is this insatiable interest in going into allocating large sums of funds (which can be utilized for a down payment of a home or a college fund) for a short presentation?

Reviewing the current marriage statistics, we might want to conduct a comparison between the current institution of marriage and today's society and lifestyles. What is the state of marriage today? According to a National Vital Statistics Report, Births, Marriages, Divorces, and Deaths: Provisional Data for October 2009 (Tejada-Vera), there were 2,077,000 marriages in the United States with a rate of 6.8 per 1000. The divorce rate was 3.4 per 1000. Close to half of all marriages ending in divorce! We understand that marriage is a great institution; however, the numbers clearly reveal that there has to be some type of adjustment or evaluation of this process.

My wife and I hold a slightly different outlook of marriage than many couples, including our friends. Traditionally, many couples believe that it is wise to remain married under almost any circumstance. Work it out! Stick with it! It will all work out, just give it some time. And my all time favorite: Don't worry. The rough times are just a part of marriage, and you will learn to deal with it. I agree with the aforementioned statements; however, my wife and I infuse the process of self and marriage evaluation. This requires a couple to ask tough questions. Are we happy in this relationship? Is this arrangement meeting the expectations of the couple/individual? Am I happy? Is my mate happy? Should we continue to stay married? Simple questions that can provide vital information concerning a marriage. We do not believe in sacrificing individual happiness and joy primarily to avoid a cultural stigma such as divorce.

I must agree that our scenario is most likely not an option for many. Removing the responsibility of raising children from our equation makes it easier for us to ask these types of questions. Please recognize that I clearly understand that if you are an individual raising two children, maintaining a household, managing your spouse and financial responsibilities, there is minimal time for the "individual." As one woman responded to a survey question: "Are you insane? Individual happiness with three children and a husband? You've got to be joking!" You are fully committed to your family and willingly placed your individual desires in a secondary position, and I applaud you for your commitment. But please do not totally disregard the idea of periodic evaluations of your life.

Close to six years into our marriage, my wife and I were faced with a matter that required our immediate attention. We were different individuals compared to our days of dating. Our individual maturity levels had increased and our individual interests, thoughts, opinions and goals were transforming. Recognizing this progress, we made a decision to infuse an evaluation process into our marriage and, fortunately, we realized that by accepting this process, we would face difficult decisions. For example, early in our marriage, my wife and I decided on a child-free lifestyle. No children? Although scorned by many, we were quite comfortable with our choice. This particular decision transpired based upon our decision to be open to self evaluation. I detail our conversation in chapter five.

Not having children in a marriage grants a couple an enormous amount of time. Without children, there are minimal distractions, and a couple is essentially forced to focus their energy toward their mate, leading to constant evaluation. With 24 hours a day to enjoy each other without the distraction of children, we made a commitment to identify activities that would allow us to work together in addition to encouraging each other to discover our individual passions. We understood that without this effort, the marriage was due to fail. From that moment forward, my wife and I committed to seeking happiness collectively and also individually through communication and self discovery. We constantly work together to achieve happiness within our marriage along with achieving individual happiness and goals. Are you happy? What is your passion? You are a beautiful person. What can I do to help you reach those goals? What motivates you? I believe in you! How can I help? In addition to the questions, I have always made it a priority to inform my wife that she is capable of accomplishing anything that she decides to pursue and encourage her to seek the most out of life. Even if, someday, her journey ceases to include me, I will not attempt to deprive her of her happiness. Her happiness and positive energy and contributions to the universe supersede my selfish wants and desires. My wife and I are true believers that each person has the right to discover truth and happiness within themselves. It is a formula that works well within our household.

Throughout this book, I constantly reference the history of the matter. Many people leap into marriage unaware of the history and statistics concerning the institution, origin of marriage traditions, history of wedding ceremony traditions, etc. There is a vast amount of information concerning the institution of marriage researched by competent scholars. In this chapter, I take a moment to touch upon just a fraction of that history and data which might be of some value.

Love and Marriage

Isn't it great when two people have the opportunity to meet at a neighborhood coffee shop on a beautiful fall morning? While sitting at a table sipping café mochas, the couple glances into each other's eyes and they smile as they enjoy their rendezvous. After a brief smile, the couple begins a conversation that will last for the next hour, which seems as if it were only a moment in time. This brief encounter is the beginning of a journey towards love and companionship, possibly resulting in marriage. Love is the cornerstone of today's relationships and the majority of us have been told by our parent(s) that we should meet someone special, fall in love and eventually get married. Surprising to many, this particular concept was not a standard until recent. For many today, it has been the belief that love has been the cornerstone of marriage since the beginning of time; however while researching the history of this great institution, I quickly discovered that a "love-based" marriage is a relatively new concept and did not surface until the late 18th century (Coontz). In previous centuries, there was little tolerance for love. In fact, love was placed low on the priority list of a marriage. If love was not the reason for marrying your companion, why were people getting married? What was the primary purpose of marriage?

Throughout history, many cultures viewed romantic love as a distraction from more important issues such as family, wealth and politics. Wealth and power, on the other hand, were more important than the emotions or intimacy of two young individuals. For example, building alliances with other families provided power, protection and legacies.

It was understood that each member of the family participated in working to make ends meet and build a future among their families. Noted by an agreement between the two families, the woman endowed all of her possessions to her husband and possessed no rights in the marriage. In fact, the woman rarely asked her mate if he loved her, and rarely did the man take interest in the wants and needs of the woman. Different cultures developed different methods in respect to love and marriage. For example, the Greeks considered romantic love as a type of insanity (Martin); in Ancient India, falling in love before marriage was viewed as a threat to the stability of the marriage; and China considered excessive love in a marriage as a threat to the alliance of the family. Under Hindu culture, love was not even considered as a valid reason to marry. Continuing to the Middle Ages, the French defined love as a derangement of the mind that could possibly be cured by sexual intercourse, either with the loved one or with a different partner. Even though the love-based marriage is quite new, I truly enjoy the experience of being in love with my wife and consider myself fortunate that she is actually in love with me. Will love survive as a foundation of marriage? I have no idea; however, I am going to enjoy this as long as it will last.

Brief History of Marriage

Ancient Greece and Rome

In Ancient Greece, marriages primarily were arranged by the parents long before the couple were formally introduced. For the woman, the parents were responsible for the arrangement of the marriage utilizing a financial arrangement in the form of a dowry. The marriage was usually considered the right of passage. The primary purpose for marriage during this period was strictly for procreation, the opportunity to gain wealth and social/political status for the families, and continuance of family heritage. The role of the wife was simply to care for her husband, raise the children and run the household. Romance was classified as secondary to practical matters or nonexistent. The average age of a girl when married was between the ages of fourteen and eighteen. The age of a man averaged close to thirty (Bennett). Women were considered inferior beings with limited rights, while men held complete control of women, children and slaves. Married men were able to participate in extramarital sexual relationships with male and female lovers, slaves and prostitutes. Married women were required to be monogamous and faced the death penalty for adultery and drinking wine. The laws pertaining to divorce made it much easier for a husband to obtain a divorce than the wife. Slaves could not marry because marriage was reserved for the privileged. Men who were single or childless were considered outcasts.

Ancient Rome considered marriage as a personal agreement between families and disregarded the need for government or religious approval (Thompson). The woman was under the custody of man who was the head of the household and children. The marriage was arranged by the father of the woman, and the consent of both individuals was required. The woman held the option to reject her chosen mate if he was morally unfit. Polygamy was a common practice, and men were not punished for adultery, while adultery by the wife was punishable by death or banishment. Parents were responsible for arranging the marriage primarily for procreation, wealth and social status. Divorce was extremely difficult and quite rare. The Roman system also utilized the dowry system.

Medieval Europe

In the early Middle Ages, many of the wedding ceremonies were conducted in the homes of the couple and included a number of witnesses. Wives were responsible for the management of the household, including child care. Early medieval Germanic wives were fortunate to have access to a number of privileges and rights and the class of elite women also controlled the religion and education in the family. In early Christianity, the Church was not supportive of marriage, but the influence of the Church concerning marriage began to increase. There was a migration of marriage law from civil to Church courts. At one point, the early Church required that all marriages be conducted in a church ceremony. Some time after this process, marriage cases were addressed in Church courts. Leo VI eventually imposed the legal obligation of the Church blessing, which led to the requirement that all marriages to be held "in the face of the Church." This action was decided upon during the Fourth Lateran Council of 1215 (Halsall), and marriage was officially declared one of the Catholic Church's sacraments. Marriages were required to display a public announcement for three weeks prior to the ceremony and must take place publicly in the presence of a priest in the front of the church. Divorce was abolished when marriage was marked as insoluble.

In the fifteenth century, a medieval Christian scholar, Friar Cherubino of Siena, created the Rules of Marriage (Okun) supporting women abuse: "When you see your wife commit an offense, don't rush at her with insults and violent blows....Scold her sharply, bully and terrify her. And if this still doesn't work...take up a stick and beat her soundly, for it is better to punish the body and correct the soul.....Readily beat her, not in rage but out of charity.....

for her soul, so that the beating will redound to your merit and her good."

Western/American

The institution of marriage in the western civilization was developed from a number of ancient cultures, such as the Roman, Germanic, and Hebrew cultures. Along with the mentioned cultures, the Christian church and the Protestant Reformation (Gray) were also strong influences. In the 16th century, the Protestant Reformation was launched as an attempt to reform the Catholic Church. As the architect of this reform, Martin Luther strongly rejected the reference by the church that marriage was a sacrament. He believed that marriage was not exclusive to Christians. Eventually, the Protestant Reformation returned marriage to a civil contract and reduced the number of marriage impediments. During the Council of Trent – The Twenty-Fourth Session in 1563 (Waterworth), the Catholic Church, responding to the Protestant movement, reconfirmed the marriage sacrament created earlier. The church demanded that a marriage not performed by the priest was considered invalid. In the 18th century, a law requiring licensing and rules of ceremonies was passed. In the 19th century, common law marriage was common in the U.S.; however, state regulation (including licensing, fees and witnesses) slowly became a part of the culture. Our existing concepts were developed from the English Common Law tradition.

Infusing Policy and Law into Marriage

When you speak with individuals today concerning the purpose or foundation of marriage, many believe that the institution of marriage is based upon religious doctrines labeled as "ordained by God." Is this belief the true origin of marriage? Does history depict this type of description? As mentioned earlier in this chapter, for centuries the institution of marriage was a private affair between a woman, man and their individual families. There were no church ceremonies, no marriage license requirements, and no laws that defined the overall process. Marriage was more of a personal and business arrangement between two families. The man and the woman were usually married in a home or the community, and the two families finalized all of the details of the relationship, such as negotiations of property. Up until the 12th century, even the Catholic Church held the belief that a marriage was solely the decision of the man and woman.

As I mentioned earlier, in 1215 during the fourth Lateran Council, marriage was defined as a sacrament by the Catholic Church. The Canons presented to the Council included verbiage that marriage was no longer a private institution and that marriages conducted in secrecy (clandestine) were forbidden by the Church, and priests were forbidden to witness those events. The Canons also stated that 1) a marriage will be considered a contract; 2) marriages must be announced publicly in the churches and conducted with a parish priest; 3) divorce was no longer allowed; and 4) marriages outside of the impediments were not recognized. If there was no opposition by the church of the marriage, the parish priest would say "I join you together in matrimony, in the name of the Father, and of the Son, and of the Holy Ghost." Responding to Martin Luther's rejection of the Catholic doctrines noted in the Protestant Reformation of the 16th century, the Catholic church confirmed its previous doctrine during the Catholic Council of Trent - The Twenty-Fourth Session, Decree on the Reformation of Marriage (Waterworth). In addition to announcing that if marriages were conducted by an individual other than a parish priest and two or three witnesses, the marriage was considered invalid.

Since this point, the institution of marriage has been consumed by a number of legal premises concerning rules and laws. For example, in 1691 in Virginia, if a white person married a person of color, the couple would be legally banished from the colony (Dorr). In the 19th Century in Britain, before the passing of the 1882 Married Women's Property

Act, the wealth of a woman was passed to her husband when married. There were a number of marriage laws adopted throughout history which are similar to the two listed above. Today, there are legal requirements such as the marriage license, prenuptial agreements, age of consent, and, of course, the financial obligations if divorced. What type of legal precedence will be placed on our children or grandchildren when they are fortunate to share their life with someone? Only time will tell.

New Economics of Marriage

Each year during football season, my friends and I gather at the neighborhood sports bar to partake in some head banging and competitive action. During our time of male bonding, regurgitation of football statistics and friendly competitive debates concerning our individual teams, periodically we would take some time to discuss issues other than sports. The subjects would range from politics or individual employment situations to women and relationships. As you can imagine, many of my friends are traditional thinking men that strongly believe in the superior role of the man in any relationship. Many of the guys are opposed to women earning higher incomes within a household, and some even believe that the corporate world has designed a global conspiracy against men by providing easier opportunities for women, which undermines the role of the man in the household. Responses such as, "Women are taking jobs from the men," or "According to my religion, the man is the head of the household" are usually the final responses in these types of discussions. I'm astonished that so many men express opinions passionately about this subject without taking a brief moment to research the subjects we discuss. For this reason alone is why I appreciate and embrace today's research tools. With these types of tools, a wealth of useful information is always available in a moment's notice. There is no reason for any person to strongly express an opinion in today's world without data to support it. I will now get to the point of this section.

Let's begin this conversation with the following fact: Fact - a larger share of women are married to men with less income and education. According to the Pew Research Center report Women, Men and the New Economics of Marriage (Taylor), over the past 40 years, considerable changes have occurred in the overall institution of marriage. Women are more educated than their spouses and the earnings of potential wives have improved at a higher percentage then their potential husbands. With these types of changes, a reversal in gender roles is at hand. This particular report also reveals data trends in marriage patterns and educational attainment by gender along with changes in economic status of adult women and men (ages 30-44, U.S. born) from 1970 to 2007:

- In 1970, 4% of husbands had spouses that exceeded their income. In 2007, 22% of husbands had spouses that exceeded their income.
- In 1970, 20% of married women had more education than their spouse. In 2007, 28% of married women had more education than their spouse.
- In 1970, 84% were married. In 2007, 60% were married.

Of course, there are a number of factors that determined the statistics, but there is no denying that there are significant changes occurring within American marriages. The gender roles are constantly being redefined and must be embraced and supported by men as we move forward.

History of Wedding Traditions

The wedding ceremony has been an integral part of our culture; however, many of us are unfamiliar with the meaning behind many of the wedding traditions. In 2009, there were over two million marriages in the U.S., and there are many (such as myself) who are not familiar with why we partake in certain acts during a particular ceremony. Why does the groom have a best man? What is the true purpose of the garter toss?

- Something Old – This good luck custom dates back to the Victorian era. Something old represents the link to the bride's past. This is usually represented by the mother or grandmother's wedding dress or a piece of antique jewelry that is a part of the bride's family; something new represents the bride's hope for a bright future and success in her new life; something borrowed represents long lasting friendships; and something blue represents love, fidelity, and loyalty (Roney).
- Wedding Ring – Ancient Egypt is recorded as the origin of the wedding ring dating back over 4,800 years using a twisted plant material (hemp) to make the ring. The circle of the ring represented mutual and immortal love. Egyptian hieroglyphics detail the use of the wedding band symbol on the walls of Egyptian tombs. The fourth finger was believed to contain a special vein which was connected directly from the heart. The Romans continued this belief and named the vein vena amoris, which is Latin for the vein of love, but they viewed the wedding band itself as a symbol of ownership (Wedding Rings).
- Wedding Bands for Men – Throughout history, men felt that there was no reason to wear a wedding band or any other symbol of marriage and commitment. This was mainly because of male dominance and the ownership

of many wives. The tradition of men wearing wedding bands was unpopular until World War II. During the war, it was popular for men to wear a wedding band to provide a reminder of their wives (Karam).

- Wedding Flowers – In ancient Rome, the bridal bouquet consisted of aromatic bunches of herbs, garlic and grains to drive away evil spirits. Later, flowers were introduced to represent fertility and fidelity (Dragon).
- Flower Girl – The role of the flower girl dates back to the Middle Ages, when she carried sheaths of wheat and herbs for blessings of prosperity and fertility. Later, the wheat was replaced by flowers. The flower girl offers a connection between childhood and womanhood (Brooks).
- The Best Man – The tradition of the best man dates back to the Germanic Goths when it was customary for a man to marry a woman from within his community. When there was a limited selection of women, men would seek a bride from neighboring communities. If the man met a bride and her family did not approve of him, the man would kidnap his bride, a practice known as "marriage by capture." When this occurred, the man would be accompanied by a male companion. Throughout the marriage ceremony, there remained a threat that the bride's family would attempt to reclaim

her, so the best man, who would be fully armed, stood by the groom providing protection. Traditionally, the bride is to the left of the groom during the ceremony. The bride was placed to the left to allow the groom to keep his right hand free to draw his sword for defense (Kidnapping the Bride).

- The Wedding Cake – Originating in ancient Rome, the marriage was sealed with a loaf of wheat bread or barley cake. The loaf was broken over the bride's head by the groom to symbolize hope for a fulfilling life and bring luck and prosperity to the married couple. The crumbs from the bread that landed on the floor were eaten by the guests and symbolized good luck for the guests (Tucker).
- The Bridal Shower – The bridal shower began as an alternative to the dowry. The belief is that the first bridal shower occurred in Holland when a young Dutch girl fell in love with a kind hearted, though poor, miller. She was not concerned with his lack of wealth; however, her father, having previously selected a groom for his daughter, rejected the marriage. The young girl was disappointed and pleaded with her father for approval, but he refused to give his blessing. The young girl chose to marry the poor miller, and her father refused to provide the dowry. The miller's friends became aware

of the young girl's situation and "showered" the bride with gifts to allow her to marry without the benefit of a traditional dowry (Bridal Shower).

- Garter Toss Ritual - The garter toss is considered one of the oldest wedding rituals. This ritual was related to demonstrating proof of the bride and groom's wedding consummation. It was common for friends and family to accompany the bride and groom to their room and obtain the garter as proof of the consummation. In addition, any article of the bride's undergarments was considered good luck, which led to groomsmen rudely attempting to remove items from the bride. To solve this problem, the wedding party had to wait outside the room and the groom would toss the garter to the wedding party (Smith).

Chapter Four

Seek Happiness at All Costs

Discover Your Passion

"Hi honey. Earlier this week, I met with Jeff Thomas for lunch. You remember Mr. Thomas from our summer trips to The Hamptons, don't you?" Dad asks.

"Yes I do, Dad," responds Lauren. "How is he?"

"He is well. He is now the dean of admissions at my alma mater and from what I understand, he is doing a great job. Here, sit," Dad says, pulling the chair for his daughter, "while I finish breakfast for you and your mother."

"Oh, this is going to be nice!" responds Lauren.

"And a total surprise," whispers mom to her daughter.

"Ladies, for your dining pleasure this morning, I have prepared a wonderful breakfast of Belgian waffles topped with whipped cream and strawberries, scrambled eggs with black

truffles, smoked salmon topped with capers, fresh coffee and, of course, mimosas. Ladies, relax and allow me to serve you today." He pours mimosas for his wife and daughter. "Now getting back to my prior thought, Jack asked about you and wondered when he would be receiving your enrollment application. As you know, Sayers University has one of the top premed and med programs in the country. I am excited about your future as a physician," Dad proudly states.

Daughter reluctantly responds "Oh that's great, Dad."

"Yes it is, dear. We have a long tradition of physicians in our family, and I will be so proud to have you part of this tradition. You will be a wonderful physician," beams Dad.

Lauren slowly takes her seat, glazing at the floor below and discreetly concealing her reaction.

Her mother notices her reaction and immediately recognizes a potential problem. "Honey," says Mom to her husband, "Can you run to the market and pick up more orange juice? We are running low and I have a feeling that a few more mimosas are in our future."

"No problem. I will return shortly," says Dad.

As the father departs from the driveway, Mom slowly reaches for her daughter's hand and says "Honey, I know that you are frustrated and your passion lies elsewhere in reference to your life goals. I recognized many years ago that your interests and talents were pulling you in a totally different direction from your father's expectations. I am here to tell you that you continue to follow your passion and I support you 100% in your career choices. It is highly important that you follow your passion and your dreams. Continue to seek happiness in all that you do concerning your career and life."

Expressing a smile of relief, Lauren responds "Thank you, mom. I assure you that I do not want to disappoint Dad, but I really enjoy writing and, one day, I'd like to write a great novel. Mom, when I am writing, it takes me to a place that is so peaceful and gratifying. Time seems to disappear when I write and my mind is full of ideas that just continue to pour out. I would really like for Dad to read some of my work, but I know that he would not be interested because of his expectations."

"I know, sweetheart but I encourage you to continue pursuing your passion for writing. Let me handle your father and we will work this out. Continue to search for the school that will offer the best education for writing and keep your eye on that novel. I can't wait to read it. You are my daughter and I just want you to be happy. Now, let's enjoy this wonderful breakfast your father prepared." states Mom.

First things first: As a woman, you are complete as you are today. You currently possess all of the positive tools and attributes needed to experience fulfillment and happiness in your life. Your journey begins with embracing the above statement. In many of my conversations with others throughout my life, I would make a point to quote the title of this chapter: Seek happiness at ALL costs. When quoting this phrase, the majority of the time I would receive quite interesting reactions such as "This guy has to be delusional" or "Waiter, I will have what he is drinking." My favorite response was always "Is that even possible?" To be honest, actually receiving a response was quite a breakthrough. My belief is that once a person responds, the possibility of evaluating the concept is quite high.

The majority of the time, the individual assumed that I was either selfish, joking, or quite unstable. Happiness at all costs? Impossible! "I would love to be totally happy in life; however, 'at all costs' is quite selfish and extreme," said one individual. "I have too many responsibilities and commitments to others in my life to seek happiness at all costs. I must compromise." I am willing to accept the previous reactions based upon the fact that many people have situations in their life that require compromise. Women are the caretakers of our children and, in many cases, the caretakers of their husbands or significant others. Still, with all of the existing challenges in life, everyone has the right to happiness.

Unfortunately, I have known only a small number of individuals that are seeking happiness at all costs. The decision to follow this path requires detailed planning and a major commitment on the part of the individual. When I have the opportunity to meet someone on this path, their energy presence is extremely high, strong, positive and engaging, and they are willing to share any information that will help better all. For example, I have a niece that is on her path to happiness. She made a decision many years ago to pursue this goal, and I am genuinely proud of this young lady. Until recently moving to a new opportunity, my niece was one of the top performers and public speakers for ZamZuu, an online home based business. This company provides opportunities for individuals who are serious and committed to seeking further improvement for themselves and their families. I've had the opportunity to watch and monitor Melissa's progress in this company and other endeavors over the last several years, and I am highly impressed. I am impressed with the fact that she is following her passion and seeking happiness at all costs. For years, I have watched her create plans and strategies for opportunities and meticulously implement her plan with impressive results. Even at times when she faced adversity, she maintained her focus and faced each challenge with strength and a smile. When I am fortunate to meet someone like this, I immediately begin to examine their patterns and their past in an effort to discover a formula. How did she get to this level of commitment in her quest?

What triggered her passion and pursuit of happiness? As a family member, what were some of the traits that my family offered early in her life that would give me any insight of her discipline?

The first task is to determine her true passion. What is her passion? Is it her ability to create a large amount of revenue? Is it her ability to build a business? In my humble opinion, no. I believe her passion is the gift or ability to inspire, the ability to assist others in reaching success in their journey. I truly believe that this is what drives her and when she is given an opportunity to help an individual become successful, this process increases her happiness. Helping others achieve their goals are the fruits of her pursuit of happiness. If you ask a number of ZamZuu participants, I believe that they will agree. For example, I am a member of Omega Psi Phi Fraternity, Inc. and I have access to all members throughout the world. I have talked with a number of my fraternity brothers of many cities who are also involved with ZamZuu and each individual expressed admiration and respect for Melissa along with a story in which Melissa provided inspiration and/or some type of assistance that improved their business. At times, I would even receive photos of the member and Melissa. In my humble opinion, these types of situations demonstrate the implementation of her true passion and pursuit of happiness. She inspires others to seek their goals in life and in return, it becomes a win/win for both parties.

Unfortunately, some individuals adamantly reject the notion of total happiness. This type of individual actually believes that suffering is a part of life and total happiness is something that is not part of God's overall plan. For example, a number of years ago I was having dinner with colleagues and the topic of happiness and suffering became the center of the conversation. As always, when I recognize an opportunity to provoke some type of analytical conversation, I rarely am able to refrain from speaking. For this particular opportunity, I happened to raise a number of simple questions: "Wouldn't it be great to live in a world of Utopia? Wouldn't it be great to live in a world where each and every person recognized their individual passion in life at the age of ten and was able to follow that passion throughout their entire life?" There was total silence at the table, coupled with expressions of skepticism and confusion. Anticipating their response, I quickly explained my questions. My reasoning was that if there were total harmony, the human race would be at its highest level of happiness, productivity and efficiency. For example, if we examine how an automobile engine functions, we know that in order for the engine to operate at the highest level, each individual part must be functioning according to its assignment or design. Without this performance, the engine will fall short of its peak. In order for this world to be a Utopia, all humans must be operating at their peak performance, which can only occur when each individual discovers his/her passion.

The group began to respond. One person thought it seemed like a great idea but wondered, "How do we make that happen?" I further explained that the first order of business is to discover our true passion in life. I strongly believe that our passion is embedded in our DNA and each person must follow their dreams and constantly seek the path of improvement and enlightenment. I believe that within each of us, there is a passion playbook and we must make it a priority to discover this trait at an early age. We must make this journey a priority. Does it seem logical to actually discover your passion during your junior year of college or at the age of 40? I deem that to be unacceptable. If each and every human on this planet discovered their individual passion in life, this world would function as a well oiled engine. Functioning at a level where all of us would be in our designated space and time in the universe would lead to the gradual dissipation, or even elimination, of day to day problems and issues.

After expressing my perspective, I noticed a look of disagreement on the face of a young lady within the group, a highly intelligent woman with a successful career in the software industry. I asked her to respond. Her response was short and brutally honest. "It is not God's plan to have a perfect world."

I have to admit, I was not quite expecting that type of response and she noticed the perplexed look on my face so she further explained her response. Her belief was that suffering improves the strength of humans and her God requires suffering which also demonstrates obedience to him. In a Utopian world-without suffering-what would we do? How would we learn or improve? It would be a boring existence. Having spent many of my childhood years in the church - and briefly as an adult – I was familiar and respected her response. After thirty minutes of dialogue, I asked the group to briefly follow my lead and dream for a moment about the possibility of each person discovering their individual passion. They agreed, so we leaped into this exercise.

What would it be like if each person on this planet not only possessed the capacity to discover their individual passion, but also the opportunity to discover this passion at an early age? Let's imagine that each human discovered their individual passion by the age of ten. In addition to the child's discovery, the child's parent(s) was able to recognize this discovery in their child and consciously make a commitment to nurture this passion throughout their youth and teen years by providing all of the required resources. What would you imagine of their childhood experience? College experience? Adult life experience? I am willing to believe that our children would be much happier, learning would be fun, communication skills would improve, the parent/child relationship would be pleasantly in sync and the child would be notably prepared for a global world. As an adult, I envision inner peace, careers that provide total satisfaction and caring/loving humans. As the exercise continued, the list of positive attributes of the simple discovery of our passion was endless.

Even as an adult, you are still entitled to this discovery. Many of us have experienced a glimpse of our passion, and the accompanying joy, at one point in our lives. A few things most likely occurred that are consistent across similar situations. First thing to note: During this discovery, the mind, body and spirit were in balance and at total peace. Second, time seemed to disappear during the activity. There never seemed to be enough time in the day to pursue or complete your task. Third, you were so focused during your activity that there was no time for negative thoughts, negative topics or negative people. Your spirit would not allow it. You did not allow trivial matters to enter your space. If you take the time to reflect on those special moments, you will vividly remember that you couldn't wait to get back to that activity and found yourself always thinking and reflecting. Immediately your self-esteem increased because you actually discovered something new about yourself. You were totally focused on the matter at hand. If you had an opportunity to experience this event each and every day for life, I believe that your life would be much more fulfilling.

My passion is what I call "bringing things to life." I enjoy dissecting a problem and discovering a solution. My inspiration in life is based upon the following quote by George Bernard Shaw: "You see things and you say 'Why?' But I dream things that never were, and I say, 'Why not?'" There have been a number of incidences when my friends approach me asking for feedback on an idea or an opportunity that they are evaluating. Even though I cannot commit to providing feedback to each and every request, I make an effort to assist with the opportunities that provide true value to the people and our planet. Once I select the opportunity, I become totally involved in the person's idea and require the same type of passion in return. This type of interaction is what I truly enjoy. Now the big question: How does every human get to this space? What is required to discover this passion?

What is Your Passion?

What is the meaning of the term passion? According to an article written by Robert Vallerand, passion is defined as a strong inclination toward an activity that individuals like, find important, and in which they invest time and energy. Each and every human has unique talents and gifts. The challenge is to discover those various gifts and, unfortunately, many individuals have been unsuccessful in their search. According to a survey by CareerBuilder.com, approximately 75% of the population is unclear of their true passion. The survey also determined that four out of five U.S. workers are not working their dream jobs. Discovering one's passion must become a priority in one's life; however, this process requires a commitment and a fundamental understanding of the journey.

Your Passion Makes a Difference in Your Well-Being

I believe that all humans agree that discovering our passion might have the capacity to improve life, but some of us are not totally convinced and require additional proof or research data. What information is available that might confirm the power of passion in our lives? Let's uncover some data. According to a recent study, Passion Does Make a Difference in People's Lives: A Look at Well-Being in Passionate and Non-Passionate Individuals (Phillippe), having a passion for a self-chosen activity makes a difference in people's lives. The study included French Canadian participants of various adult ages: early adulthood (18-22 years), adulthood (23-30 years), middle-age (31-50 years), and later adulthood (>51 years). The study concluded that it is not only a single aspect of an activity that makes it beneficial for well-being, but whether the activity itself is engaged in passionately or not. The findings also concluded that the type of passion one has for an activity matters with respect to a person's well-being. The study was based upon three types of passion: harmonious passion, obsessive passion and non-passionate people. While harmonious passion entails control of the activity and a harmonious coexistence of the passionate activity with other activities in identity, obsessive passion entails the relative lack of control over the passionate activity and conflict with other activities in one's life. Individuals with harmonious passion experience positive emotions and better concentration and experience high levels of well-being during and after engaging in a passionate activity. Individuals that experience obsessive passion feel that they must engage in the activity that they love. Due to internal forces, the passionate activity takes disproportionate importance and interferes with other activities of the person's life. Harmonious passion becomes an important focus and it makes us better communicators.

Harmoniously passionate people registered at a much higher rate than obsessive passion and non-passionate people concerning hedonic and eudaimonic well-being. In addition, harmoniously passionate people demonstrated a significant increase in vitality over a one-year period while obsessively passionate participants showed a slight decrease and non-passionate participants an even larger decrease (study 2). Results continued to prove that passion was shown to be relatively stable and able to contribute equally to well-being across all adult life stages from ages 18 to 90 years.

Passion affects men and women of all ages, which indicates that harmonious passion might help to preserve or even increase older adults' well-being. While the mere activity engagement does not necessarily guarantee an increase in well-being, retaining a harmonious passion toward a self-chosen activity may represent the most effective way to reach such a goal.

How Do I Begin to Discover My Passion?

We are constantly told to "discover your passion." For many, this task can be difficult and may require a type of road map or instruction manual to begin the process. How do we discover our passion or purpose? According to Carol Dweck, we must begin by asking ourselves a number of questions, reflect on those questions/answers, document our life's experiences and implement a few daily routines. Below are a few suggestions that might help to launch your journey of self discovery.

Questions List:
What did you want to be when you were a child?
If money was not a factor, what would you want to do each day of your life?

Task List:	
Be sensitive to moments that reveal inspiration.	Talk with people who have expertise in your areas of interest.
Constantly brainstorm. Become curious.	Talk with others concerning their passion path.
Be open to learn from others.	Define what you love about yourself.
Research, Research.	Never give up!
Engage in meditation or prayer.	Create a list of your best talents.
Try different things. Experiment.	Begin to eliminate your fears.

Character Strengths and Virtues

Christopher Peterson and Martin Seligman of the VIA Institute of Character developed the VIA methodology that identifies and classifies the positive psychological traits of human beings. Character Strengths and Virtues (CSV) classification identifies six classes of core virtues that link with positive psychology which includes 24 measurable character strengths. Mr. Seligman and Peterson have determined that a part of achieving happiness is tied to understanding your strengths and the ability to improve your strengths.

- Wisdom and Knowledge – strengths that involve acquisition and use of knowledge
- Courage – strengths that allow one to accomplish goals in the face of opposition
- Humanity – strengths of tending and befriending others
- Justice – strengths that build a healthy community
- Temperance – strengths that protect against excess
- Transcendence – strengths that produce connections to the larger universe and provide meaning

In addition, Peterson also examined the gender variances of the 24 character strengths utilizing a survey. His results disclosed the leading strengths of women included all of the virtues along with three of the core strengths: gratitude, curiosity and the capacity to love and be loved. Below is a chart that details each strength and virtue:

VIRTUE	CHARACTER STRENGTH	DEMONSTRATION
Humanity	Capacity to love and be loved	You value close relationships and are able to share reciprocal caring with others.
	Kindness	You tend to be generous and are nurturing and helpful to others.
Wisdom	Curiosity	You're fascinated by a lot of topics and are open to new experiences.
	Love of Learning	You systematically strive to add to what you know, either on your own or through formal study.
	Critical thinking and open-mindedness	You think things through, examining them from all sides. You're able to change your mind in light of new evidence.

Justice	Fairness	You believe in giving everyone a fair chance and tend not to let personal feelings become a bias.
Courage	Integrity	You speak the truth and take personal responsibility for your feelings and actions.
Transcendence	Gratitude	You are aware of the good things in life and take time to express thanks.
	Appreciation of beauty and excellence	You look for and value the beauty in all aspects of life, from sunsets to fine foods.

What is Happiness / Hedonic Adaptation

Many think happiness is based upon your status or the accumulation of things, such as extravagant homes, luxury cars, country club memberships, designer clothes, etc. Many studies, however, have proven that the above listed items are not the foundation of happiness. Please understand that there is nothing wrong with wanting or having these types of things. I am willing to admit my desire for the finer things in life, but we must be aware that the purchase of an item will not sustain happiness. According to Merriam-Webster's Online Dictionary, happiness is defined as a state of well-being and contentment; a pleasurable or satisfying experience.

Many people think that they know what will make them happy, though studies have shown that there is a difference between what they think will make them happy and what actually provides happiness. Being able to predict what will give us happiness is not as easy as it seems and, unfortunately, we are not doing well with our predictions. One of the human traits that is a component is our ability to quickly adapt, which is parallel with hedonic adaptation. When we encounter a new experience, this change only temporarily impacts happiness but quickly diminishes as we become accustomed to that particular experience or as stated the ability to adapt (Frederick). When a person reaches each material based goal, he or she seems to never be happy with that what we have. Hedonic is defined as "devoted to pleasure." Studies have indicated that regardless of what we face in our lives, happiness is a relatively constant state. For example, there have been a number of studies conducted that demonstrate the decline in happiness among lottery winners. What we should be truly seeking is what is termed Hedonic treadmill which is the tendency of a person to remain at a relatively stable level of happiness despite changes in fortune or the achievement of major goals.

Happiness Promoting Activities

What types of activities are available to promote happiness? Positive psychologist researchers (Lyubomirsky) have identified a number of methods to increase happiness in one's life. They are listed below:

- Kindness Activity – Document a plan to be kind to others. Determine at a minimum three types of kindness to perform regularly.
- Optimism Activity – Write about our best possible selves. Spend 20 to 30 minutes writing about a future in which everything turns out the way you hoped. Identify and change automatic pessimistic thoughts.
- Gratitude Activity – Keep a gratitude journal. Communicate to other people that you are grateful to him/her.
- Avoid Over-Thinking – Avoid situations that cause over-thinking. Write your thoughts in a journal. Don't get caught up in over-thinking situations that lead to unhappiness.
- Cultivate Social Relationships – Commit to making time for relationships. Verbally express your excitement

concerning your friends' success, and verbally express sincere admiration and appreciation.

- Developing Strategies for Coping – You must be able to manage stress. Attempt to see things clearly. Solve problems by dividing the problem into manageable components. Look for meaning in the situation.
- Learn to Forgive Others – Document situations that might suggest forgiveness. Appreciate being forgiven. Imagine forgiving another. Write a letter of forgiveness. Practice empathy.
- Savor Life's Joys – Be appreciative during daily activities. Reminisce with others. Replay happy events to yourself. Celebrate good news.
- Commit to Your Goals – Extensive research indicates that goals provide a sense of purpose, improve self-esteem, and add structure to our lives. Pick goals that have meaning to you and create a desirable outcome. Pick goals that require unending activity. Select goals that complement each other.
- Practice Religion or Spirituality – Research indicates that practicing religion or spirituality improves long-term health and creates happiness. If you choose to practice religion and/or spirituality, seek meaning and purpose in God, enlightenment, art or science. Develop the ability to see a higher consciousness in things.

- Take Care of Your Body – Meditate. Be physically active. Act as a happy person.

Does Money Make You Happy?

Make no mistake, we are a materialistic society; however, it has been well documented and proven that it is highly unlikely that an increase of standard of living will increase our happiness. According to economists and sociologists, standard of living has increased dramatically over the years, but happiness has not matched the increase of standard of living. The relationship of happiness and money is minimal. For example, if you won a $250 million lottery today, shouldn't you be happy for the remainder of your life? Can't the money buy you happiness? Researchers have determined that a certain amount of money can make us happy; however, happiness does not continue to increase in proportion to income. Over the past few decades, there has been enormous economic growth in many countries and minor increases in happiness. In a two part study (Brickman) that included a sample of 22 lottery winners of $50,000 to $1 million, researchers discovered that the lottery winners experienced an initial emotional high, but within a year returned to their previous level of happiness. The results indicated that winning the lottery did not make people happier. There was also a comparison of lottery winners and individuals that did not win the lottery. There was no significant difference in their levels of happiness. In America, the personal income has more than doubled over the last 50 years, but happiness levels have remained flat (Myers).

Psychologist David Myers, author of The Pursuit of Happiness, states that the material things do not create happiness. Once people adapt to a certain level of wealth, new increments of things are required to "rejoice the joy." A survey (Diener) of 49 of the Forbes richest individuals determined that 37% reported happiness levels lower than average. There is, however, a money/happiness connection. Mr. Ed Diener documents that happy people tend to have higher incomes later in their lives, suggesting that happiness may help increase your income.

Declining Happiness Among Women?

One of the most gratifying things about writing this book is discovering a wealth of information that I can utilize to become a better person. I discovered a paper entitled The Paradox of Declining Female Happiness (Stevenson). Stop! This cannot be true! What is this about? We should be moving toward happiness, not the opposite. What could possibly be the cause of this decline? My initial hypothesis: Women are discovering that their intellectual, spiritual and mental levels are consistently increasing at a far greater pace than to men. Recognizing this occurrence and sticking to their traditional beliefs concerning the current leader role of the man, the woman feels that she must reduce her progression to appease the head of the household. Women are frustrated because we, as men, are not taking the initiative toward constant growth. Again, the above is simply my thoughts concerning the decline. Let's review the data.

By measuring the subjective well-being of men and women across a number of datasets, this paper reveals that over the last 40 years, women's happiness has declined both absolute and relative to men, regardless of salaries, marital status, race, parental status, or age. This has occurred even with the vast improvements among the lives of women during this period. Examining data collected by the General Social Survey, Stevenson and Wolfers compiled a wealth of evidence concerning subjective well-being by gender in the United States and other industrialized countries. One of the measurement tools of subjective well-being was simply a question to respondents: "Taken all together, how would you say things are these days? Would you say that you are very happy, pretty happy, or not too happy?" Additional questions concerning their satisfaction with a number of aspects of their life including work, marriage, and children were also posed.

What is causing this disconnect? In reality, there are a number of theories that indicate the possible causes of this decrease in women's happiness; scholars continue to debate this issue. Quite frankly, I was reluctant to include the above data in this book, but having a total perspective of any subject matter is essential. So let me make a suggestion on how to utilize this information. First, you must acknowledge and respect the research data. There have been a number of proven surveys, evaluations, etc. referencing this subject and the research is on-going. Second, utilize the existing data for self-evaluation. Take some time to read different studies, reports, or findings in reference to the decline of happiness and determine what may be applicable to you. Third, if there are any possible comparisons, make a conscious effort to address the issue. Begin to ask yourself tough questions and commit to change. Seek happiness at all costs!

Positive Psychology

Throughout history, psychology as a discipline has focused on the negative aspects of the human mind, i.e. anger, grief, sadness and anxiety. Fortunately, this study has led to a number of breakthroughs in understanding psychological disorders. Conversely, there are a number of scholars concentrating on the opposite end of this spectrum named positive psychology. According to Martin Seligman, founder of Positive Psychology and psychologist at University of Pennsylvania, positive psychology is the scientific study of what makes people happy, what makes life fulfilling and the role of positive emotions in the human psyche or the study of human behavior, life satisfaction, and feelings of well-being. Challenge negative thoughts, play to your strengths, seek out meaning in your life, count your blessings.

From a general sense, what are the primary tenets of this particular discipline? Defined by Dr. Seligman, positive psychology has three main branches:

- Positive Emotions – the study of contentment with the past, happiness in the present, and hope for the future;
- Positive Individual Traits – study of the strengths and virtues, such as the capacity for love and work, courage, compassion, resilience, creativity, curiosity, integrity, self-knowledge, moderation, self-control, and wisdom; and
- Positive Institutions – the study of the strengths that foster better communities, such as justice, responsibility, civility, parenting, nurturance, work ethic, leadership, teamwork, purpose, and tolerance.

In addition to the above list, there are three components that contribute to an individual's happiness (Seligman):

- Genetic Set Point - an individual's natural level of happiness such as some people are naturally happier than others. The genetic set point of happiness comes from inherited genetics and childhood upbringing. Studies have determined that the genetic set point represents 50% of an individual's overall happiness.
- Life Circumstances - includes a wide range of factors such as relationship situations, individual's health, and financial situations. Studies indicate that circumstances are responsible for 10% of an individual's happiness.
- Intentional Activities or Happiness Promoting Activities - things an individual can do that create feelings of happiness. Intentional Activities are responsible for 40% of an individual's overall happiness.

Chapter Five

Do I Really Want Children?

Are Children a Requirement?

"Ladies, we have been shopping the entire afternoon. I need FOOD!" exclaims Jennifer to her friends.

"Well, let's be naughty today. Let's not count calories. Let's not think about our daily workout routines. Let's pig out! Are we all in?" asks Carie.

In unison, the ladies shout "YES, WE ARE IN!"

"Well, ladies, pick your poison," says Carie.

Alison happily responds "I am going to have a nice juicy foot long hot dog loaded with chili, cheese and onions."

"I am in on that selection," says Jennifer. "I am going to load my hot dog with spicy mustard and a lot of sauerkraut. Yummy!"

Finally Carie responds, "I have a taste for a large slice of pizza with the works: pepperoni, mushrooms, Italian sausage, extra cheese, onions, tomatoes and jalapeno peppers on a thick crust. I say we finish our meal with a brownie covered in ice cream and chocolate sauce"

"Well ladies," shouts Jennifer, "Let's do this!"

As they were eating, Carie gazes at a mother and her child walking by the restaurant and says "I can't wait to have children. I can't wait to spend Saturday afternoons shopping with my two beautiful girls, staying up late on a Friday watching movies and eating junk food, attending their recitals and school plays, and taking family vacations."

"Oh yes," agrees Jennifer, "I'd like a boy and a girl. I look forward to little league baseball games and working on science projects with my son and playing with dolls and helping my daughter prepare for her campaign speech when she runs for the president of her high school student council." They joyfully laughed, dreaming about their future.

"Alison, what are your plans?" asks Jennifer. Alison pauses and softly replies "I am not sure that I want children." The entire table goes silent and Carie and Jennifer have surprised looks on their faces.

"What are you saying?" asks Carie. "Are you serious?"

"Yes I am," responds Alison. "I've thought about this for awhile and I am comfortable with my decision. I have many reasons why, and I am perfectly at peace with my choice. Besides,

there are many children that I can share my love and time with through my life. Love is universal and fulfilling no matter who the child may be. I am at peace with my decision. Who knows, I might change my mind in the future. But for now, there will be no children," explains Alison.

"Are you serious?" asks Carie. "You've got to have children. You will make a great mommy. This is what we have talked about since we were kids: go to college, graduate, get married, have children and live happily ever after as neighbors in the suburbs. That was the plan."

"Yeah, Alison," states Jennifer, "No offense but how can you be so selfish? I mean, you are very intelligent and you would be a great mommy. What are you thinking?"

"I totally understand your reaction," says Alison. "My decision does not go along with our plans, but we have been friends for many years and I would love for my best friends to accept and support my choice. Is that possible?"

"Alison, even though we don't understand your decision, we love you and support your decision on this matter. We are friends for life," says Carie. "Now let's pig out and get back to our shopping!"

Having a child is truly one of life's greatest blessings. First birthday parties; fathers walking their sons on the first day of school; mothers taking pictures of their daughters before their first prom; fathers giving their daughter's hand in marriage – these experiences are truly fulfilling for many.

I was extremely fortunate as a child. I thank the creator each day for my parents. As I reached adulthood, I often wondered how my parents were able to take on a daunting task. We all know that it couldn't have been easy.

Unfortunately, many children were unable to experience the type of love we received as children and continue to receive. Many children experience poverty, abuse, crime and neglect. There are even adults that are addressing issues that occurred during childhood within a dysfunctional environment. How do we begin to confront these types of issues? One suggestion is that all adults considering bringing a child into this world should make it a priority to become familiar with the current and future state of children, not just locally but globally.

When evaluating the possibility of bringing a child into this world, we must first take a close look in the mirror and truthfully determine if this is something that we truly desire. We must examine the long list of items required to correctly and efficiently raise a child. We must look at world poverty levels, health, homelessness, education and other factors that threaten the well being of a child.

Do I really want a child? Do I really want the responsibility of a child? These are great questions to ask. If you choose to have a child or not to have a child, either option is entirely acceptable. Any type of conscious discussion concerning having children will be beneficial today, tomorrow and a number of years into the future. In any event, the bottom line is that you must be comfortable with your decision. Allowing others or societal norms to influence your decision may not lead to a sound solution. At the end of the day, you will be responsible for rearing your child.

Early in our marriage, my wife and I decided on a childfree lifestyle. After carefully evaluating the responsibilities of rearing a child and honestly asking ourselves if we truly wanted children, we made our decision. Even when I reflect on our dating days, children were rarely the topic. That is quite unusual. Many individuals make it a point to research the intentions of a mate before the wedding ceremony. Our conversations mainly centered around our careers and just enjoying life. We never asked, "Do you want a boy or a girl?" or "How many children would you like?" This subject was not discussed. Even though children were not discussed before we were married, at that time we both automatically assumed that having children was "the thing to do" in a marriage.

A few months after our wedding, I vividly remember our first discussion concerning children. We talked specifically about when would be the right time to have children. Should it be within the first year of our marriage or should we wait? How many children? Boy or girl? We covered the standard "baby" questions. Victoria's response was quite forthright: Time line? No preference; Number of kids? No baseball team; Boy or girl? Definitely a girl! The selection of gender was her only requirement. Allow me to explain. The gender criteria was based upon my wife's history. My wife's mother died when she was three years of age. To this day, she misses her as if her mother was in her life for many years. For those that have lost their mother, I believe that you truly understand her emptiness. Even though she was fortunate to have a stepmother who is extremely important in her life, there has always been a void in her life. Deprived from experiencing many years of special moments with her biological mother, she misses her so much.

Having lost her mother, she always believed that if she had a daughter, she could somehow create moments that could possibly construct a connection with her mother. For example, she imagined herself and our daughter having lunch on a beautiful Saturday afternoon casually discussing "girly" subjects and also believing, with all of her heart, that her mother was in their presence, laughing and loving along with them. She imagined a time when our daughter would ask for motherly advice and imagined the advice that her mother would provide. This connection was important to her. To this day, she and I strongly believe that her mother is with her at all times and continues to watch over her. My wife wanted a girl to possibly create for her daughter the precious moments that she missed with her mother.

At the end of our discussion, we reached an agreement concerning the time line. Let's wait at least two years before we start a family. That gives us time to discuss the other details and spend a little quality time together before we leaped into parenthood. We wanted to simply date for the first two years. No commitments, no babysitters, no soccer games, no piano recitals. Just time to ourselves. Two years into our marriage, it was time to revisit our plan. We scheduled a dinner date specifically to discuss this matter. I actually remember our order. For me, prime rib, medium rare, garlic mashed potatoes, salad and a glass of Cabernet Sauvignon. For my wife, a grilled chicken salad with a slice of toasted bread topped with cheese. After ordering a glass of wine and our entrees, we began our discussion with our initial plans of having at least one child. Before we talked about the details, I brought up one simple question: "What if we actually decided not to have children?" No Children?! How can we not have children? Our parents would kill us! What will our friends say? Who is going to take care of us when we are old? We have to have children! Once we purged all of the typical questions and concerns, we sat at our table and looked at each other in silence. After a moment, we realized that the thought of not having children had never been considered as an option. Each one of us was taught that marriage and children were a given in life.

What would it actually be like to live childfree? We visualized our lives without children and wondered about the possibilities and experiences. Our first evaluation was strictly from a financial point of view. No day care costs. No cost for diapers and formula. No cost for clothes, private school or college tuition. We enjoyed the sound of that. Next on the list? The commitment factor: no late nights of crying, no endless hours of homework, no headaches concerning discipline. The list was endless. We decided to order more wine to close our conversation and I asked the question one more time: What if we actually decided not to have children? We were unsure if it was the thought of not having children or the three glasses of wine that gave us a warm feeling throughout our bodies while discussing this subject. Whatever it might have been, it was quite pleasing and my wife began to wrap her thoughts around this possibility. One month later, we officially made the decision to remain childfree.

Now don't think that we ruled out the possibility of having children from that point forward. The subject was not totally dismissed for a lifetime. We agreed to revisit the subject each year on our anniversary for at least five years. We chose five years because of our age. We were both 28 years of age when we were married and did not want to have a child well into our thirties. During each annual evaluation period, we talked with individuals and couples from various age groups concerning their decision to have or not to have children. We received a wealth of feedback and advice and continue to have this conversation with others even today. After the five years, our decision to remain childfree stood strong and we were truly at peace with our decision. To this day, we continue to stand behind our decision and feel that it was the best decision for our relationship.

As I stated earlier in this chapter, if someone is contemplating having children, the emotion factor must be removed from the equation, and that person must commit to asking tough questions. In making this type of decision, again, it would be in the best interest of an individual or couple to understand the current global condition of children.

Facts Concerning Children

As parents or future parents, I think that it is a good practice to be aware of the overall world population of children. Below are just a few facts. According to the U.S. Census Bureau – International Data Base, the world population by age is as follows:

Age 0-4 (614,773,311)
Age 5-9 (595,018,990)
Age 10-14 (595,775,079)

Total world population: 1,805,567,380 (Age 0-14)

According to the Federal Interagency Forum on Child and Family Statistics, in 2008, there were 73.9 million children in the United States (Age 0-14). 1.6 million more than in 2000. Projected numbers are 82 million in 2021. In 2008, there were approximately equal numbers of children in three age groups: 0-5 (25 million), 6-11 (24 million), and 12-17 (25 million). Birth rate in the United States dropped 2% in 2008, which was the biggest drop in 40 years. This gives us a foundation to move forward with the information that follows.

State of the World's Children

With a global outlook, major advancements in technology and many travel options available, each one of us can be sensitive to world situations. No matter where we live, we are all affected by global circumstances, and we all can make some type of a difference. In order to become better humans, our global awareness of events and various issues must be a part of our thinking. All individuals must come together as one on a global scale to address issues concerning children and their mothers. The information below is provided by The World Health Organization, the World Bank and UNICEF which have joined together to develop a framework that is detailed in The State of the World's Children 2011 report.

Why am I discussing this issue of global initiatives? Just for a second, imagine that you are a mother living in a country where many children die before the age of five from causes that are easily treatable in most developed countries. Continue to imagine that today, with all of the available resources, there is a high rate of children dying simply from a sickness that you and I take for granted in the United States. If we are a part of the group of fortunate individuals who have a wealth of opportunities and resources, it is our responsibility to be aware of global situations, not just those in our backyard. We must participate in this process of improving the lives of all children. So let's examine what is being implemented and/or developed to address global issues.

In 2000, the United Nations, along with many of the world's leading scientists, academia, international financial institutions, development specialists, economists, and politicians, developed a set of goals that embody basic human rights and needs that every individual should be able to enjoy. The Millennium Development Goals (MDGs) consist of eight goals that address the world's primary development challenges. The MDGs, which were designed to be achieved by 2015, were created from action and target items contained in the Millennium Declaration, adopted by 189 nations and signed by 147 government and heads of state during the Millennium Summit in 2000. Each goal is listed below and, as you will notice, a huge portion of the goals address the wellbeing of children:

- Goal 1: Eradicate Extreme Poverty and Hunger
  Target 1a – Reduce by half, by 2015, the proportion of people whose income is less than $1 a day
  Target 1b – Reduce by half, by 2015, the proportion of people who suffer from hunger
- Goal 2: Achieve Universal Primary Education
  Target 2a – Ensure that children everywhere, boys and girls alike, will be able to complete a full course of primary schooling
- Goal 3: Promote Gender Equality and Empower Women
  Target 3a – Eliminate gender disparity in primary and secondary education in all levels of education no later than the year 2015

- Goal 4: Reduce child mortality

  Target 4a – Reduce by two-thirds the under-five mortality rate
- Goal 5: Improve maternal health

  Target 5a – Reduce by three-quarters the maternal mortality ratio
- Goal 6: Combat HIV/AIDS, malaria and other diseases

  Target 6a – Have halted by 2015 and begun to reverse the spread of HIV/AIDS

  Target 6b – Have halted by 2015 and begun to reverse the incidence of malaria and other major diseases
- Goal 7: Ensure environmental sustainability

  Target 7a - Integrate the principles of sustainable development into country policies and programs; reverse loss of environmental resources

  Target 7b – Achieve a significant improvement, by 2020, in the lives of at least 100 million slum dwellers
- Goal 8: Develop a Global Partnership for Development

  Target 8a - Develop further an open, rule-based, predictable, non-discriminatory trading and financial system (includes a commitment to good governance, development and poverty reduction)

  Target 8b - Address the special needs of the Least Developed Countries (includes tariff- and quota-free access for Least Developed Countries' exports, enhanced program of debt relief for heavily indebted poor countries (HIPCs) and cancellation of official bilateral debt; and more generous official development assistance for countries committed to poverty reduction)

Target 8c - Address the special needs of landlocked developing countries and small island developing states (through the Program of Action for the Sustainable Development of Small Island Developing States and the 22nd General Assembly provisions)

Target 8d - Deal comprehensively with the debt problems of developing countries through national and international measures in order to make debt sustainable in the long term

Target 8e – In cooperation with developing countries, develop and implement strategies for decent and productive work for youth

Target 8f – In cooperation with pharmaceutical companies, provide access to affordable essential drugs in developing countries

Target 8g – In cooperation with the private sector, make available the benefits of new technologies, especially information and communications technologies

The project listed above is just one of many currently implementing solutions that address global concerns. When we make a choice to have a child, awareness of our global surroundings will benefit your child and other children. As your child is growing, sharing the experiences of children from other areas of the world will develop a compassionate and caring child.

Why Do You Want Children?

As I talked with many women, both with and without children, I asked "Why do you want children?" I was not surprised to discover that many women honestly believed that having children was their duty. Having children is the foundation of their existence. In their upbringing, it was constantly emphasized and understood that children were to be a part of their lives. As my wife and I experienced, the thought of not having children never occurred.

Procreation is definitely important and is guaranteed to continue, and there are many other reasons why adults choose to have children in addition to populating the planet. What are your true reasons for having children? According to Bernard Berelson's essay, The Value of Children: A Taxonomical Essay, he demonstrates that each individual reason can be placed one of six categories: biological, cultural, political, economic, familial, and personal. As mentioned earlier, many people feel that it is a civic duty to perpetuate the population or that children become the standard within a culture. In some situations, having children becomes an economic consideration. Other reasons include 1) children continue a family's blood line; 2) couples have children because of problems in their relationship and they feel that having a child will solve or fix the problem; 3) children offer unconditional love toward the parent(s) which provides a sense of being needed or empowerment for the parent(s); or 4) requirement for religious reasons/beliefs. There are many reasons why individuals choose to have children. In determining your reason for bringing a child into this world, please be clear that your primary reason should be the well being of your child.

Father's Participation in Rearing Children

In many societies, mothers typically provide the primary parenting and responsibility for children and the fathers are labeled as helpers (Arendell). Even though there have been major strides concerning the participation of the father, it is important for a woman to address a few questions with a potential mate before having a child. How does the man feel about children? How involved do you want your mate to be in raising your child? Is your mate prepared to assist with the little things in child rearing such as changing a diaper, waking at 3 a.m. when the child is awake or sick, or even preparing food and bottles for the child? What is the role of a father in reference to raising your children? How does your mate define his particular role? There are a number of questions that you can ask before you begin a lifelong commitment. A simple question such as the number of children becomes relevant. If his response is one and you number is three, you might have an issue. The questions above are simple and informative and should be addressed before moving forward.

It is to your advantage to seek answers. If you are a woman who is planning to be a full-time mother and your mate is the breadwinner, a lot of time and effort might not be required from your mate. If you are, however, a career-oriented woman or someone who anticipates a certain amount if child rearing assistance from your partner, you might want to conduct a fact finding mission or an informal interview to determine just how much effort that person is willing to invest. For example, it is a possibility that your mate was part of an environment in which there was no requirement to participate in household duties. It is possible that this person was nurtured the majority of his life by his mother and possibly sisters. Or it might be someone who believes that it is the responsibility of the woman to devote herself to the child's needs. There are a number of reasons that should persuade a woman to become curious about her partner's belief system or family history when talking of children. You must not assume that a mate will automatically transform into a super dad the moment your child enters this world. It is most likely that your mate's past and current habits and traits will continue after your child is born.

What are some of today's overall statistics concerning fathers' participation in caring for their children? How much time is the father extending in caring for his children? Unfortunately, there is far less research data available addressing the father's involvement of raising children compared to the woman's role. However there are a number of studies being conducted to explore the father's role. For example, according to data referenced in Changing Rhythms of America Family Life (Bianchi), married fathers averaged 6.5 hours per week caring for their children in 2000, which was a 153 percent increase since 1965. The results from An American Time Use Survey from 2003-2004 confirmed that fathers with working wives spend more time as primary caregivers for their children than fathers with nonworking wives. If you take a moment to ask a father about the percentage of his involvement in raising children compared to women, most likely he will boldly declare that the percentages are close to even. Fifty-fifty split! He is always there when needed. But, according to the paper American Families (Bianchi), mothers are more likely than fathers to report that the mother is the individual that does the majority of the parenting. Findings concluded that mothers stated that the mother is the main disciplinarian of children (47 percent, compared with 17 percent), the mother is the one who plays with the children (37 percent, compared with 14 percent), the mother provides most of the emotional support for children (45 percent, compared with 24 percent), the mother monitors the play friends (51 percent, compared to 27 percent), and the mother provides the majority of basic care (70 percent, compared to 58 percent). With women pursuing careers, obtaining advanced education degrees, changing philosophies of the institution of marriage, family life, and independence, what is the thinking of men and their roles within this new frontier? After interviewing a number of men, I found the majority of married men expressed that the role of raising a child is the responsibility of the mother. When asked about the percentage of care provided within the relationship, men felt that women were responsible for more than 50% of child rearing, such as 1) physically caring for the child and 2) emotionally committing to the child. With the current accomplishments of women, they are expecting men to step up to a more engaging role in parenthood.

Childlessness Today

Being childless in today's society can be difficult for a woman. Many people immediately assume the worst when they discover that a woman is without children. Unfortunately, a large percentage of individuals are unaware of the many reasons why a mother is childless. Childlessness can occur by choice or by a situation where a woman has no control of being childless. There are a number of designations defining the term childless. According to the National Survey of Family Growth, childless women of the United States are labeled as temporarily childless, voluntarily childless (childfree), or nonvoluntarily childless. Temporary childless is defined as women who expect to have one of more children in the future. Voluntarily childless women are defined as women who are physically able to have a birth and expect to have no children in their lifetimes or they are surgically sterile for contraceptive reasons. Nonvoluntarily childless women are defined as women who expect to have no children in their lifetimes, and either have impaired production or are surgically sterile for reasons other than contraception. In 2002, among the 61.6 million women 15-44 years of age, 42 percent were childless. Within that percentage, 33 percent were temporarily childless, 6.2 percent voluntarily childless, and 2.5 percent nonvoluntarily childless. The 6.2 percent of women who were voluntarily childless in 2002 is up from 4.9 percent in 1982.

Despite the reason of childlessness in a woman's life, the number of childless women is constantly rising according to a report released in 2010 by the Pew Research Center titled Childlessness Up Among All Women; Down Among Women with Advanced Degrees (Livingston). The number of childless women (United States) in their early forties has risen since the 1970s. Approximately one in five American women by ages 40-44 is childless compared to the trend in the 1970s when one in ten women was childless ages 40-44. Among all women ages 40-44, 18% in 2008 has never given birth opposed to 10% in 1976. Addressing race and ethnic groups, figures show that 20% of white women are childless compared with 17% of black women and Hispanic women and 16% of Asian women. Since 1994, childless rates have grown more rapidly for black and Hispanic women, three times the rate of white women. Women who have never married are more than likely to be childless; however, their rates have declined over the past decade. Childlessness has fallen over the past decade for women with advanced degrees.

As I mentioned earlier, there has always been an issue with the perception of childlessness however the negative perception of childlessness is decreasing. The number of adults who disagree that people without children "lead empty lives" rose to 59% in 2002 from 39% in 1988. The attitude that children are the central component to a good marriage has also changed. According to a Pew Research

Center survey 2007 (Taylor), 41% of adults responded that children are very important for a successful marriage, as opposed to 65% of adults in 1990.

Childless rates among women born in 1960 in other developed nations are similar to the United States (Trends) according to the Organisation for Economic Co-operation and Development. Please note below:

International Childless Rates - Women born in 1960	
Country	*Childless Rate*
United Kingdom	22%
Finland, Netherlands	19%
Ireland, Italy, United States	17%
Belgium, Denmark, Norway, Spain, Sweden	12%-14%

Childless By Choice

In the United States and abroad, there is a growing trend among women and couples not to have children or to be what is called childfree, childless by choice or voluntarily childless (Casey). Childfree is the term used to describe individuals who desire not to have children. Unfortunately, being childfree is frowned upon by many people in society. Many studies have revealed that many voluntary childless women are typically viewed by others as selfish, materialistic, abnormal, egotistic, unfeminine, immature and even deviant. Many childfree women or couples have experienced situations in which there is a direct attack concerning their choice. Opposing the social norm can attract a number of offensive looks and abrasive comments from mothers, family members, friends and individuals within your ingroup. What people fail to realize is that there are many reasons why women are choosing a childfree lifestyle. This type of decision can be linked to one or more of the following: the increase of career options for women, available opportunities for higher education, various forms of birth control available, and the emphasis and awareness on women's rights. In reference to education, most studies have determined that education levels clearly influence the decision to be voluntarily childless.

As I stated earlier, my wife and I are in the category of voluntary childless. Even after twenty years of marriage, we continue to receive negative feedback concerning our decision and lifestyle. Let me rephrase that. We receive negative feedback primarily from women concerning our childfree status. Some of the responses consisted of "You should have children. The two of you would be great parents" or one of my favorites "Who is going to care for you when you get old?" Then there's a quite distasteful response directed at my wife is "It is natural for a woman to have a child. You will feel so empty without a child." Fortunately, at the end of the day, it is completely your decision to select a childless lifestyle. From the beginning of time, many women and couples have decided to remain childfree.

Reasons for a Childfree Decision

Why would a woman or couple not want to have the gift of life? Why would someone who is a good person and would be a great parent not have children? Well according to Childfree by choice: a review (Agrillo), there seems to be a number of reasons for the childfree choice:

- The lack of desire to be a parent (the primary reason for me and my wife)
- Dislike of the behavior of children
- Contentment with the enjoyment of pets
- Lack of interest in conforming to the social obligations
- Personal advancement such as not wanting to sacrifice privacy/personal space and time for children
- Not wanting to commit to financial responsibility
- Belief that having one or more children would reduce career advancement
- Perceived or actual incapacity to be a responsible parent
- Physical and health concerns, including concern for safety of child, the risk that an existing medical condition may affect the child's care and future

If you take the time to clearly examine the list above, many will most likely identify one or two items that you actually considered before becoming a parent. Unfortunately, there are many people who believe that these types of concerns will just disappear the moment the child arrives. It is not that simple.

Childfree and Religion

The majority of humans on this planet adhere to some type of religious belief. Each form of religion provides a foundation that primarily governs your lifestyle. With that being the case, is there a direct connection between a religion's core belief system and having children? As a member of your religious group, is it a requirement to have children? Would you lose favor with your creator if you choose not to have children? I strongly believe that many members of organized religion have not even asked these types of questions to their leadership. If you were in a marriage counseling session and you informed your minister, priest, or rabbi that you and your mate have decided to remain childless, how would your spiritual leader respond? Would you lose favor with the members of your religious group if you choose a childfree lifestyle? It is important to understand your religion's overall stance concerning procreation within your faith. Is having a child a blessing or a command?

Is it an option for a Christian couple to choose a child-free lifestyle? My research has discovered a number of beliefs among leaders within Christianity. There were ministers who believe that it was not a sin to choose childfree and ministers who were strongly opposed to childfree Christians. For example, according to Albert Mohler, writer of an article titled Deliberate Childlessness: Moral Rebellion With a New Face, "Christians must recognize that this rebellion against parenthood represents nothing less than an absolute revolt against God's design. The Scripture points to barrenness as a great curse and children as a divine gift." In an article written by Lon Adams, he says "Biblically speaking, we can't ignore the fact that God considers parenthood an incredible blessing." He states that the Bible does not reference any scripture that references childlessness and that the Bible never envisioned married couples deciding against parenthood. He also references Genesis 1:28, "Be fruitful and increase in number; fill the earth and subdue it." He maintains that Christians who ignore this specific command are rejecting God's design for humanity.

An article written by John B. Shea, MD, for the Catholic Insight, says, "The Church teaching clearly does not allow spouses to avoid having children simply because they don't want them. Reproductive freedom is contrary to the teaching of the Church. Those unwanted children have great value in the eyes of God." If you are a part of a belief or religious system, please make it a point to ask your leadership about this subject. Even if it is for an educational purpose, it is beneficial to have a clear understanding.

Finances Required to Raise a Child

Now let's get back to the numbers. Numbers never lie! Why is it that when a decision is made to have a child, so many people conveniently disregard the overall financial requirement and commitment? As an infant, what is the cost of diapers, clothes, and food? How much will a child need to attend college? Will you be able to provide a child with the best elementary and secondary education possible? Why does your child need an Xbox and a Playstation? Strap yourself to your seat and digest the numbers below!

According to the U.S. Department of Agriculture, a baby born today will cost between $150,000 to $250,000 to raise from birth to age 18 (Lino). A middle-income family will require more than $250,000 to raise a child from birth to age 18. In addition to the above mentioned amount, you also must include the cost of other items such as private school and the cost of college, which will be an additional $100,000 to $300,000. The amounts above include diapers, feeding your child, child care, clothing, toys, extracurricular activities, additional health insurance and much more. As an infant, the cost of disposable diapers is an estimated $100 per month along with and additional $100 for baby formula. Childcare can be estimated at $100 a week per child. A delivery is estimated to cost from $10,000 to $30,000 for those without insurance. If your child requires special treatment such as treatment associated with premature birth or other health problems, neonatal costs can approach up to $200,000, depending upon the specific situation. If you have a child with special needs, your out-of-pocket costs will be increased and can range from $560 to $970 annually. In addition to direct costs, children will require additional living space, which means a larger home, higher utility costs, and higher insurance premiums.

Chapter Six

Don't Live in a Box

Travel the World!

"Hi Jackie. Thanks for inviting me to dinner. I was so excited when I got your call. What's on the menu tonight?" asks Deb.

"Well, first do me a favor and grab a bottle of Chianti from the wine cellar and let's get this evening started. We will start off with fried calamari and fried zucchini and for our entrées, you have a choice between stuffed veal chops over spinach with mushrooms in a wine sauce or Mediterranean sea bass with asparagus and roasted potatoes sautéed in a garlic wine sauce."

"Wow it is going to be a tough decision choosing my entrée," says Deb.

"Well, let's do this! Why don't we just place both entrées on the table and we will enjoy them both," Jackie suggests.

"Sounds like a winner to me. Let's get this thing started. Let's

enjoy this wine," says Deb. "Now Jackie, what is up with you? Every few months, for about a week, you just disappear off the face of the earth. No one can get you on the phone, you don't respond to text messages or email and we do not see you at the spa. What is going on with you?" asks Deb.

Jackie responds, "Girl, my husband and I made a decision last year to make some changes in our life. We made a commitment to travel abroad at least two to three times per year. Neither one of us ever had a chance to travel abroad and we have always been interested. So we made it happen. Last month, we took a two week trip to the Greek Isles and, let me tell you, we had a great time. I mean the opportunity to experience a different culture and people was an eye opener and a life changing experience for me. Just taking the time to sit and communicate with someone from a totally different world was something that I will always cherish because it immediately gives you a different perspective. You begin to compare backgrounds and realize that there are a lot of opportunities to learn when you travel the world. Six months before Greece, we traveled to Paris for a short excursion. Of course, you can imagine how romantic that trip turned out. We have planned our next three trips. On our next trip, we are traveling to Tokyo, and I am picking up a little of the Japanese language for the trip. Then it will be Egypt to check out the Pyramids and then Rio. Not only are we learning new things and meeting interesting people, my husband and I are more close now than we have ever been. We are even taking a French class together, and you know that is a stretch for my husband. Deb, you have got to take some time to visit the world. You will not regret it. There are so many things that you will experience that will make an impact in your life," explains Jackie.

"Wow, I had no idea that you were traveling the world. International travel has always been something that I wanted to do. Maybe we can plan a trip with just the girls," says Deb.

"That sounds like a great idea, Deb. Let's make it happen," says Jackie.

Deb responds, "I will toast to that plan!" as they raise their wine glasses and toast to their future travels.

If you talk to many of your friends and ask if they would like to travel the world, most likely you will get an resounding YES. A vast majority of people would enjoy visiting other countries to experience the beautiful lands, local people and cultures. Who wouldn't want to view the city of Paris from the Eiffel Tower, sit at the base of The Great Pyramid at Giza in Egypt, take a river cruise on the Thames River in London, visit the Acropolis in Greece, or even ride an elephant on safari in South Africa?

Unfortunately, my wife and I have not traveled internationally as extensively as I would like, but we have decided that travel will be a major priority in our lives moving forward. In order to prepare for our travel destinations, we make it a point to research various locations and talk with a number of individuals who have experienced international travel. For example, I have a good friend who has actually traveled to over 90 percent of the countries on this earth, and the travel was unrelated to business. He is an engineer and, for a number of years, his employment assignment was in Saudi Arabia. Each year for their vacation, he and his wife would choose a number of countries to visit and continued this routine for many years. The couple craved the opportunity to visit many destinations and interact with people from different backgrounds. They both have exceptional communication skills and the passion to embrace all people and cultures. His wife, Anna, is a beautiful vivacious woman from the island of Tonga in the Pacific. She was a nurse also working in Saudi Arabia when they actually met.

When visiting the United States, it was customary for him and his wife to visit our home in Atlanta for at least a weekend. Our weekend routine was quite simple and unfortunately short. The couple would usually arrive in Atlanta on a Friday afternoon, and I was responsible for picking them up at Hartsfield airport. We would return to our home and relax a bit while adjusting to the Atlanta time zone. After a little rest and relaxation, it was time for a martini (or two) while discussing our dinner plans.

For our dinner engagement, it was a tradition to select an international cuisine that represented one of the countries that Darrell and Anna had a chance to visit. This process allowed an opportunity for the visiting couple to share their experience, along with a brief education session. For instance, one year Darrell insisted that we have dinner at an Ethiopian restaurant. Victoria and I were excited because the actual dinner was a learning experience which included enjoying the cuisine and the stories detailing their adventures in Ethiopia. They would begin by describing the food on the menu. Darrell would generally order a number of native drinks and a number of dishes so each person could experience each entrée. For example, he explained that the traditional Ethiopian cuisine consisted of various meat dishes, spicy vegetables and a thick stew served on top of a flatbread named injera. When eating the various dishes, utensils were not required. We held the injera in our fingers and used it to pick up each bite of food.

Once the order was taken, the stories would begin. It was like a symphony when the two would begin to share their ventures, spanning from the taxi ride to the airport to the day of their return. With both Darrell and his wife being highly animated, each moment was an experience my wife and I would savor. Along with the stories, Darrell and Anna would make it a point to engage the restaurant staff by inquiring about their homeland. Within seconds, both parties were sharing similar experiences. It was though Darrell and Anna provided a connection to their home. At times, Darrell would even speak their native language. Dinner was truly an experience and treat on multiple levels. After dinner, we would visit a local watering hole, and the stories would continue.

The following morning, Darrell and I had our own routine. We were early risers and our wives always enjoyed sleeping in after a long night of good food, conversation and libations. Our Saturday morning would begin with the breakfast of champions: Bloody Marys and a cigar for our morning appetizer, followed by a traditional breakfast of scrambled eggs, sausage, hash browns, and toast. Darrell and I would have breakfast on the patio and discuss the business at hand. For the ladies, when they decided to grace us with their presence, we would prepare mimosas to accompany their breakfast. Throughout our friendship, we both realized that it would be in our best interest to eventually launch some type of business. Our assignment was to carefully craft a plan for this venture. Beginning with a whiteboard session, our set-up consisted of a world map, pins and notepads. Our primary goal was to identify possible business opportunities in the countries that they visited that particular year. With only the weekend to meet,

I made it a point to research the history, current numbers, economic conditions, and primary resources of that particular country, which allowed us to cover more topics without having to take time to educate me on the basics of that particular country. To begin the session, Darrell would place a pin on the map identifying the country and, if available, photos of their visit. From that point, he would give a brief description of his experience in that particular country, particularly with respect to possible business opportunities. We would continue until we exhausted all opportunities available in that particular country.

Today, Darrell and Anna are divorced; however, they are great friends and we continue to enjoy our weekend experiences. Currently, Darrell is on an international assignment, and my wife and I look forward to actually meeting him in a number of destinations to get hands on experience of a number of different cultures.

Why Should We Travel?

For many years, traveling has been available only to the wealthy. In addition, many of us live in close proximity to our family or a spouse's family, essentially confining our travel. We spend the majority of our lives missing out on what this beautiful planet has to offer. Fortunately, travel has become extremely convenient and affordable, allowing each person an opportunity to expand his or her horizons. With a little effort, opportunities abound!

We all dream of traveling, but we assume that it is unaffordable and quickly discount many opportunities. Sometimes we assume that it is unsafe in other areas of the world, allowing fear to impede us from travel. If we would carefully take a second to research the number of available destinations on this beautiful earth, it just might pique your interest to further evaluate your travel options. First, let's take a look at some of the facts concerning our beautiful planet in order to get an overall understanding of what we might be missing:

- According to the World Bank, the world population has reached 7 billion people.
- There are seven continents on earth – Africa, Antarctica, Asia, Australia, Europe, North America, and South America.
- According to the U.S. Department of State, there are 194 independent countries around the world.
- There are over 6,000 different languages spoken in the world today. Close to 200 languages have a million or more native speakers.
- Over the past six decades, tourism has experienced continued growth and diversification to become one of the largest and fastest growing economic sectors.

- By 2020, international arrivals are expected to reach 1.6 billion (World Tourism).
- The overall export income generated by international tourism reached $1.1 trillion in 2008 (World Tourism).
- There are 22 major religions of the world.

The earth is an enormous place, and there are numerous opportunities to experience. Your options are endless.

Why should we travel? Why should I board a flight and travel more than fifteen hours to South Africa? What value is it to sit at a café in Sidney while holding a conversation with a local citizen? Why should I go through this hassle? There is a coffee shop less than a block from my residence. Why does anyone go through the hassle? According to the World Tourism Organization WTO, travel has three popular benefits: learning and discovery, rest and relaxation, and nurturing family and friendship ties. From a simple weekend getaway to an extended vacation abroad, there are endless benefits. Traveling offers many opportunities for discovery, and studies have proven that individuals are given an opportunity to learn about the people and culture of that particular region. With this connection, people discover similarities, history, and cultural backgrounds of the groups which in turn provide an opportunity to widen our perspective and enrich our lives. From a psychological perspective, travel is also relaxing and revitalizing. With today's stressful careers or long hours spent raising a family, a short weekend trip has been proven as a great way to take a break and actually prepare for the upcoming tedious week. Traveling also offers an opportunity to spend quality time with your family and friends and create a lifetime of memories.

You Are In Control

Many firms in the travel industry have clearly recognized the importance of you, the customer. For years, the travel industry offered minimal options to customers, but with increasing control on the part of the customer, the travel industry determined that a major adjustment was required and continues to make adjustments to provide a much better travel experience. There are many studies, surveys and information available to the travel industry which provides a more personal experience for you, the customer. For instance, there are a number of reports that provide valuable customer data to the travel industry such as Measuring Guest Satisfaction and Competitive Position in the Hospitality and Tourism Industry: An Application of Stance-Shift Analysis to Travel Blog Narratives (Crotts). In addition, there are a number of research documents and articles available specifically referencing women, such as The Gender Gap in Travel: Myths and Revelations (Kugel).

Also included are a number of nonprofit organizations that concentrate specifically on travel, such as the Travel and Tourism Research Association (TTRA). This organization is committed to improving the travel industry through education and publications. So as a traveler, the industry is set up to assure that you have the best travel experience possible.

Travel has also been transformed by the Web. Technology has taken a major role in the industry, allowing the customer to research and schedule travel at any time and take advantage of available deals. Self serving travel sites offer search capabilities at your convenience and the option to compare costs for various options on a number of destinations and types of getaways without the requirement of sales agents. You are in control!

Women and Travel

Over the past 20 years, research shows that women are a large percentage of travelers, especially business travelers. A report provided by The Herman Group stated that in 2007, 43% of business travelers worldwide were women. The U. S. Travel Association estimates that 32 million single American women traveled at least once last year. Out of 34 million travelers who traveled alone in the past three years, 47 % were women, and women make up 52% of adventure travelers. It is also estimated that women will spend close to $125 billion on travel in the next year (Bond). With this data available, the travel industry quickly recognized the value of women travelers.

In an April 2009 article in the Marketing to Women newsletter, EPM Communications reported that nearly all hotel executives say their outreach efforts are gender-neutral; however, they added that women's preferences are important considerations since women act as the key decision-maker in 70% of travel plans. For women, travel options and possibilities are endless. In addition to business travel, more women are taking advantage of leisure travel. The industry has developed a number of increasingly popular women-only vacation packages, ranging from spa weekends to adventure trips. In addition, there are a number of women's travel groups that offer travel deals, regularly scheduled trips, and women travel tips. Women-only getaways have increased drastically, and the travel industry is meeting this need.

The travel industry has made a conscious effort to develop a number of accommodations and services exclusively for women. For example, The Hyatt Regency offers a series of wellness education and healthy living retreats, and Wyndham Worldwide offers a program named Women on Their Way, an online resource dedicated to female travelers.

There are also options such as women-only hotel rooms (along with entire hotel floors for women) that provide amenities, such as healthy meal options, oversized bathtubs, bath salts, gourmet coffees and teas, yoga mats, and women's books and magazines. Other amenities include women-only fitness centers and rooms with hand creams and skin moisturizers. Aesthetic features include improved lighting, bathroom counters that are conducive to makeup application, and branded aromatherapy products. The industry has also added many resources enhancing security for women. According to a survey conducted by American Express concerning women's travel, 84 percent of females are generally more concerned about safety and security than men when traveling. As mentioned earlier, many hotels are responding to security issues by offering female only floors; background checks on hotel personnel; hotel staff escorts to their room; key card access; better lighting throughout the facility; female-only staff and a number of other safety controls.

Importance of Host Culture / Intercultural Communication Skills

As I discussed earlier in this chapter, there is an importance of international travel. When coming in contact with different cultures, we discover different value systems and beliefs. Learning about different values not only broadens our thinking but also enriches our own value system. Even though it has been proven that tourism broadens your thinking, various studies have revealed that many forms of tourism do not engage in cross-cultural interaction which offers a better understanding between the tourists and hosts (Jaworski). There is a wealth of research concerning the motives of tourists confirming the primary reasons why people travel abroad which include relaxation, scenery, sport, and nature to name a few. Only a small percentage of their interests, however, are directed toward cultural learning. With this behavior, the tourist misses out on the lifetime experience of genuine intercultural contact. There is limited contact between tourists and local people. Unfortunately, much of the contact with the local people is categorized under the role of servants or helpers (Jaworski). This type of reaction occurs because of socialization, or more specific, primary socialization (Bochner).

Primary socialization is defined as a process through which people, early in their lives, learn the core values of a specific culture. Core values, typically, are highly resistant to change. This becomes an issue when interacting with a different culture (host culture) and not respecting the host culture's way of life. We shut down and immediately stand on the beliefs of our particular culture.

In order to solve this problem, when we travel and encounter different culture systems, we must develop or improve what is called intercultural communication skills. By just applying a number of intercultural communication techniques, you can increase the joy of your trip tremendously. According to Psychology Wiki, there are a number of ways to improve communication when facing unequal language skills such as:

- Research the culture and communication customs of that culture.
- Listen closely without judging. If you do not understand, request confirmation of understanding.
- Respect the local communication styles.
- Avoid using your culture's slang.
- Before entering into communication with the host culture, research the host culture's perception of your culture by reading literature that the host culture distributes concerning your culture.
- Learn greetings in the host culture's language.

The simple suggestions listed above will earn the respect of the host culture which will in turn increase your interaction and provide a more enjoyable vacation. There are a number of Intercultural Training and Assessment tools that you can experience that will be valuable to your preparation.

Financial Importance of Tourism to International Destinations

If you've traveled abroad, you probably have encountered native individuals selling products and/or services. What many of us fail to realize is that the selling of local goods and services is extremely important to the well-being of that particular destination and its people. For many countries, tourism is a primary instrument for regional development.

According to the World Tourism Organization, a specialized agency of the United Nations and the leading international organization in the field of tourism, the definition of a tourist is a visitor whose length of stay exceeds 24 hours in a location away from home and whose main incentive for travel is other than financial. When you travel, tourism offers a variety of economic impacts for the visiting destination, including tax revenues, retail trade, transportation, restaurants, lodging, amusements, and employment. Secondary economic impacts can include an increase in property taxes. Tourism is even utilized as a tool to address poverty in the world by the World Tourism Organization. This organization utilizes the Millennium Development Goals (MDGs) detailed in Chapter 5. The UNWHO believes that tourism can play a significant role in the eradication of poverty throughout this world. The United Nations appointed the World Tourism Organization to develop a program that would maximize tourism as a central driver of economic development and growth. The UNWTO created The Sustainable Tourism-Eliminating Poverty (ST-EP) program to address this issue. To date, UNWTO has implemented over 90 ST-EP projects in 31 countries.

According to the UNWTO, tourism accounts for 45% of the exports of services of least developed countries and is a major job creator for many of the world's most vulnerable populations. In 2009, emerging economies received $306 billion in international tourism receipts (36% of the global total) and 410 million international tourism arrivals (47% of the global total). With such a powerful impact, the tourism industry plays a considerable role in the achievement of Millennium Development Goals 1, 3, 7 and 8.

Top International Tourism Destinations

Referencing the World Tourism Organization, the following ten countries were the top international tourism destinations from 2007 to 2009. I think that it is time to contribute to the overall number of International Tourist Arrivals for the next 30 years. There are a number of great destinations on the following list.

Top International Tourism Destinations			
Rank	*Country*	*International Tourist Arrivals (2009)*	*International Tourist Arrivals (2010)*
1	France	76.8 million	76.8 million
2	United States	55.0 million	59.7 million
3	China	50.9 million	55.7 million
4	Spain	52.2 million	52.7 million
5	Italy	43.2 million	43.6 million
6	United Kingdom	28.2 million	28.1 million
7	Turkey	25.5 million	27.0 million
8	Germany	24.2 million	26.9 million
9	Malaysia	23.6 million	24.6 million
10	Mexico	21.5 million	22.4 million

It's a big world! Travel is becoming more inexpensive and I am sure that you have a number of friends that would enjoy each journey. Pack your bags and broaden your horizons. The world is waiting. Will you join me?

Chapter Seven

The Human Genome Project:

The Beginning of the End of Prejudice

"Hi mom," says Sarah over the phone.

"Hey sweetheart. How are you today?" responds her mother.

"I am well," responds Sarah. "Do you have time for lunch today?"

"Of course, I have time to have lunch with my daughter! Do you have a place in mind?" asks mom.

"Yes, there is a great café that recently opened in the art district. It's located on the corner of 5th and Arts Avenue. Does noon work for you?" asks Sarah.

Mom responds "Perfect. I will see you there. Love you!"

"Great, I love you too!" says Sarah.

Sarah and her mom meet at the restaurant. After they are seated, the waiter asks "Ladies, may I take your order?"

Sarah responds "Yes, I will start with the shrimp and crawfish croquettes, and for my entrée, I will have grilled yellowfin tuna with roasted potatoes."

Mom follows, "I will start with Oysters Rockefeller, a half dozen, and a bowl of your fresh crab soup. For my entrée, I will have your delicious Crawfish Etouffee, and for dessert, I think I will have the Chocolate Hazelnut Torte with the cherry sauce."

Thank you ladies," says the waiter, "your order will be out shortly."

"Having dessert today, mom?" says Sarah. "You deserve it, so enjoy."

As they casually enjoyed their lunch, Sarah briefly mentioned that she had something to discuss with her mother. Taking a deep breath she says "Mom, I have to talk to you about something."

"What is it?" asks Mom.

Sarah responds, "I understand that our family has a strong tradition and history, and we are committed to sustaining that history. But I must confess that I have not followed that tradition and have broken one of the unspoken rules. I am dating someone that the family would most likely have trouble accepting."

"Honey you know that you can always talk to me. Please help me understand your situation."

"To be honest, I am dating a wonderful guy that treats me with total respect, holds me close when I am having a bad day, has a sense of humor, and loves me dearly." says Sarah.

"He seems to be a winner. What's the problem?" asks Mom.

"He is black," says Sarah. Mom quietly sits back in her seat, briefly gazes out of the café window and takes in the news. Sarah allows her mother to sit quietly for a few seconds as she processes the information that was just given to her. Her mother nervously takes a sip of her drink and attempts to prepare the appropriate words to respond to her daughter's comments.

"Honey, first of all, I love you and I will always respect your decisions in life and I thank you for loving me enough to come to me in confidence; however, your father and our family will be the issue."

"Yes I am fully aware of that," says Sarah.

"You know that your father and our families believe that blacks are different. I understand that our beliefs are archaic, but that's just the way it's been for many years. This is something that I should discuss with your father alone before you make an attempt to explain."

"No!" says Sarah, "I need to be the one who gives him this information and I would like for you to be with me."

"Now that is the strong, intelligent daughter that I raised. Of course I will be there to support you. Call your father and let's deal with this together," says Mom.

"I love you, Mom" says Sarah.

"I love you too, sweetheart. We will get through this situation together as a family."

Please forgive me, but I really feel that this information is important to all. I know you are asking, "What is this Genome thing? Why are we discussing DNA in the midst of content that references personal enlightenment?" Your questions are valid and perhaps the subject might seem not to belong; however, if you allow me to explain, I promise that I will provide some clarity and you will grasp the importance of the Genome content. Before I discuss my point, let me give you some insight concerning my introduction to this subject and also provide a high level understanding of genome and DNA.

The Genome Project was introduced to me through one of my mentors. Actually, it is the gentleman mentioned in Chapter One. His reasoning for introducing me to this subject was solely to inform me that the Genome Project has proven scientifically that all humans are the same. His reason for introducing me to this project pertains to his life project named Our Republic Walk. Our Republic Walk proposes implementing the notion of "We The People," noted in the Constitution of the United States. His project consists of bringing all Americans together to create a citizen movement toward a national Republic. The core tenets of Our Republic Walk are 1) foundation of a Republic is based on freedom; 2) respect for others and their views of others; and 3) the placement of the interest of all above self interest. He is quite discouraged that the majority of people in this country are unaware of their citizenship rights, unfortunately allowing the government to act in their own interest opposed to the best interest of the people. His initial goal is to get people to come together as one voice for the betterment of the people. The results from the Human Genome Project are one of the primary tools used to justify his overall goals and strategy. Now let's briefly explain this Genome project.

The Human Genome Project

The Human Genome Project (HGP) formally began in 1990 and was a 13-year international scientific research project coordinated by the U.S. Department of Energy and the National Institutes of Health. The primary goal of the project was to "map the genes in human DNA" or to begin to understand the blueprint of a human. This project, which ended in 2003, was instrumental in further understanding the structure of the human DNA, which will have a major impact on life sciences, medicine, and biotechnology. What are some of the fundamentals of DNA and genome? I will only discuss three important components: cells, human genomes and DNA.

What is a cell? Cells are the basic building blocks of all living organisms. It is the smallest unit of life that is classified as a living thing. There are trillions of cells in the human body. Each cell contains instructions needed to keep your body functioning, including brain functionality, blood flow, and muscle growth. The instructions of each cell are contained within a molecule called DNA, or deoxyribonucleic acid. DNA is the container for all instructions needed to maintain cells. A genome is simply a complete set of DNA instructions.

Now that we've got the technical jargon complete, let's get to my point: According to the National Human Genome Research Institute, the genomes of any two people are more than 99% the same. Having proven that all humans are basically the same in design, there is little, if any, room for the justification of prejudicial behavior. The argument that people are different based upon the color of a person's skin is invalid. With just that fact alone, we can begin or continue our fight to remove prejudice from our societies. This chapter concentrates solely on examining basic individual prejudicial tendencies. Before we can begin to address this deadly social disease, we must first become familiar with a number of basic facts followed by self examination. I promise that this process will lead to a better person, which, in turn, will foster better relationships with all people of this beautiful earth.

I am by no means attempting to present an overall theory that solves this problem. Fortunately for all of us, there are a number of individuals and organizations that are committed to addressing this problem on many levels. My goal is to simply provide a number of fundamentals addressing prejudice, which will possibly become a part of our daily fabric. In order for humans to continue to evolve, it is a proven fact that we must work together as one cohesive group. We must set aside all forms of prejudice and hatred toward people based upon their gender, color of their skin, body size or any other physical feature. Prejudice and the behavior that it leads to continues to be a major stumbling block of the continuance of human evolution. In order to eradicate this disease, we must first evaluate ourselves concerning our individual prejudices.

"An extraterrestrial visitor examining the
differences among human societies would
find those differences trivial compared to the similarities.
We are one species."

Carl Sagan

Defining Prejudicial Behavior

Most individuals are familiar with and have dealt with some type of prejudice in their lifetime, and many of you probably feel that you know a lot about the subject. As an

African American male, my family and I are well aware and have experienced many types of prejudice. The Merriam-Webster Dictionary provides the following definition of prejudice: preconceived judgment or opinion; an adverse opinion or learning formed without just grounds or before sufficient knowledge; an instance of such judgment or opinion; an irrational attitude of hostility directed against an individual, a group, a race, or supposed characteristics. There are many definitions of prejudice, but most reference the fact that prejudice nature is rooted in judgment that is without basis in facts.

As stated earlier, many have experienced some level of prejudice in our lifetime and unfortunately for some, the memory of specific events has been difficult to erase. For example, close to ten years ago during a Thanksgiving holiday celebration, my mother shared a personal story. In 1968 in Illinois, my mother and many others in our community were extremely active in the civil rights movement led by principles developed by Dr. Martin Luther King, Jr. As leaders of the local NAACP, my mother and father were true believers of the non-violent movement and traditional Christian principles.

Similar to many families during a Thanksgiving holiday, our family routine consists of a lot food, a little rest, more food, and more rest. After dinner, we lounge around the host's home for the remainder of the day, usually talking about each other and discussing family matters so the Atlanta family members can catch up on events at home.

This particular year, I asked my mother a number of questions in reference to defining moments in her life. During that conversation, I asked her to tell me about an event in her life that created extreme anger. This event could be related to the category of her choosing. What event really tested her faith? As I anticipated, she immediately responded. This event from 1968 was so vivid in her mind that there was no reason to take time to think about a response. She knew exactly the event, time and place as if it occurred the previous week.

She began to explain that she was grocery shopping in one of the local stores. As she was making her traditional stroll through the store purchasing groceries for a household of seven, a somber announcement came over the store's intercom system. The announcement was short and to the point. "May I have your attention please, your attention please? I am sorry to announce that Dr. Martin Luther King, Jr. was assassinated today in Memphis, TN. Again, Dr. Martin Luther King, Jr. was assassinated today in Memphis, TN." My mother stated that she immediately stopped and was physically unable to move forward. She began to cry and at that moment, she heard the voice of a white man standing not far from her. Laughingly he said, "It's about time they got that nigger!"

Already distraught from the announcement, her faith was truly tested at that moment. In order to stay true to her beliefs and recognize the current atmosphere of that era, she felt that it would be wise not to respond and immediately exit from the store, leaving her basket of groceries in the middle of the aisle. Even today, I believe that the pain of that day is deeply rooted in her memory, however, she continues to be a fighter of prejudice and injustice. She will never end her fight and expects her children to follow her lead. We all have made the commitment.

Let's establish a clear baseline of prejudiced behavior throughout our history. Women were unable to vote until 1918; Jews murdered during World War II by the Nazis; large scale racial discrimination occurred against African Americans during the Civil Rights Era; ethnic cleansing in Darfar, Bosnia and Kosovo; widespread violence against lesbians and gays; societal prejudice against the elderly; constant stigmatization of the obese; and the assumption that all Muslims are terrorists. This is just a microcosm of events that have occurred just within the last century. We must become sensitive to prejudicial situations in our daily routines in order to recognize these patterns and address or correct when needed.

Types of Prejudice

In order to confront prejudice, it is a requirement to understand its many forms. From personal discrimination to institution prejudice, we face bias on a daily basis. It is imperative that we refrain from disregarding various types of prejudice as if though they are nonexistent. For example, one of the primary obstacles of understanding prejudice is that the majority of individuals are still under the impression that racism is the only type of prejudice. Unfortunately, this is far from the truth. There are a number of types of prejudice individuals encounter on a daily basis. Let's examine a partial list below:

- Racism – the belief that race accounts for differences in human character or ability; belief that a particular race is superior to others.
- Ageism – prejudice or discrimination against a particular age group, especially the elderly.
- Sexism – the prejudiced attitude and/or discriminatory behavior based on the presumed inferiority or difference of women as a group.
- Homophobia – irrational fear of, aversion to, or discrimination against homosexuality or homosexuals.
- Religious prejudice – discrimination against an individual or group because of their individual religious belief system.

- Prejudice against People with Disabilities – a prejudgment about individuals with disabilities and discrimination against individuals with disabilities.
- Nationalism – belief that a particular nation and its people, culture and values are superior to those of other nations.
- Economic Classism – exploitation on the basis of socio-economic class, individual behaviors along with systems of policies and practices established to benefit the upper class while degrading the lower class.

Levels of Prejudice

There are a number of levels of negative behaviors resulting from prejudice that individuals may encounter. These levels can range from a simple act of telling an ethnic joke amongst friends during a dinner party to an inhuman attempt to exterminate a people. Gordon Allport, considered one of the premier experts addressing the subject of prejudice, created a scale that details a range of activities that may occur because of prejudice. Allport's Scale of Prejudice consists of five points which detail a broad range of activities set in motion by prejudicial beliefs. Even though the early stages of the scale seem quite harmless, these types of activities can spur later stage activities. We must never discount situations we label as harmless.

- Scale 1: Antilocution – Considered the lowest degree of prejudice, this particular level defines individuals that normally speak of prejudices about a disliked people amongst their friends opposed to speaking directly to the target subject(s). Rarely are these verbal remarks expressed outside of their circle of friends. Subjects are usually discussed within an environment where a particular group gathers in private.
- Scale 2: Avoidance - Avoidance is defined as a situation in which the individual with the prejudice nature avoids the disliked group. The individual might even avoid certain situations or locations, even to the extent of inconvenience. Considered to be harmless initially because there is no direct contact with the disliked group, evidence establishes the posture for possibly reaching the next level of prejudice.
- Scale 3: Discrimination – There is a conscious effort to exclude the disliked group from certain areas of society, such as neighborhoods, employment opportunities, educational opportunities, or a number of methods of social control. Segregation is defined as a method of discrimination with the enforced separation of two different groups, such as blacks and whites in the United States up until the late twentieth century.

- Scale 4: Physical Attack – When prejudice reaches this level, acts of violence or the threat of violence occur against the disliked group. Acts of violence, such as destruction of the group's property, physical harm to members of the disliked group, or even lynchings or murder, happen at this level.
- Scale 5: Extermination – This represents the ultimate degree of prejudice. Extermination is the attempt to permanently remove a large number or all of the population of the disliked group. Examples include massacres, genocide, or ethnic cleansing of a people.

I venture to believe that each one of us has experienced an incident categorized within at least three of the scales above. Allport's scale is just an additional tool we can utilize to improve our awareness of prejudice that surrounds us daily.

Origin of Prejudice in an Individual

How did we get to a point in which a particular individual wishes negative actions on another individual based solely on a human trait or belief? How is it that the human has not evolved to a point to where we are able to clearly recognize the wrong in a particular prejudiced act? Are humans born prejudiced? Does our prejudice nature originate from the DNA of our parents? Clearly not. Prejudice is directly formed and influenced by inner group experiences (various family members, friends, groups and surroundings) throughout an individual's life. For example, if each one of us would take a moment to reflect on our childhood and try to remember a possible incident when we either overheard our parent(s) or certain family members talking or were actually taught about a certain type of people from our inner group, we will most likely discover this behavior occurring a time or two. I personally recall a number of incidents when I heard a family conversation in which the subject matter influenced my belief system, based solely upon the fact that it was stated by a family member.

According to many experts, the human is not born prejudiced; however, prejudice usually occurs at an early age. There have been a number of studies that have proven that a young individual forms prejudices even before their introduction to individuals outside of their inner group. Psychologists and sociologists have discovered that the adult personality is developed by the age of five based upon individual childhood experiences. Conversations among family members during a family barbecue, listening to adult conversations during a Friday night dinner, or even receiving advice from your grandparents while visiting on a spring weekend, instill prejudices into our children. Accordingly, without a conscious effort, prejudices are difficult to reverse. For example, I am sure that the majority of you are familiar with the black doll-white doll social experiment that was first conducted in 1954 by Dr. Kenneth and Dr. Mamie Clark. This experiment consisted of 1) placing a black baby doll and a white baby doll on a table and 2) asking a number of children between the ages of 3-7 to select the doll that they preferred. The majority of children chose the white doll. As of today, a form of this experiment has been conducted by a number of different groups and the results are quite similar. The doll choice of each child was influenced by the belief system of their inner surroundings. Adults must be very careful when communicating with our children during their formative years.

Unintentional and Intentional Prejudice

There is extensive research on the subject of prejudice. A number of brilliant individuals have committed an enormous amount of time and energy to studying this dilemma within human nature. During my research, I happened to discover a scholar who provides information that can help us understand two core components of prejudice. Dr. Jim Cole, a psychologist and human relations consultant in Washington State, defines two types of learned prejudices with which we must become familiar: unintentional prejudice (implicit) and intentional prejudice (explicit). Unintentional prejudice or early learning is defined as: a learned stereotype early in life; learning that is not challenged or tested; unlikely to change without awareness training. Intentional prejudice or later learning is defined as: learned stereotype later in life; inability to empathize with other people's feelings; an active learning process; an integral part of an individual's identity. Developed by Dr. Cole, below is a chart that identifies the differences between the two types of prejudice:

	Unintentional Prejudice	**Intentional Prejudice**
Time of Learning	Early Learning	Later Learning
Learning Process	Passive acceptance of information	Active learning process
Distribution in Population	Almost universal	Less common
Motivational Strength for Prejudicial Behavior	Weak to none	Strong
Maintenance Dynamics	Lack of awareness Practice without re-evaluation	Strong connection to personal identity
Respond to Political Changes	No	Yes

	Unintentional Prejudice	**Intentional Prejudice**
Conditions for Response	When a person is preoccupied	When a person feels threatened
Integration with Other Beliefs	Not necessary Possible vestigial behavior	Style of approaching world and environment
Response to Confrontation	If behavior is in conflict with intentional beliefs, then guilt might result Possible denial, Possible defensive reaction	No guilt Possible denial Possible defensive reaction
Recommended Treatment or Intervention	Gently increase awareness through discussion Show acceptance for individual Practice to create new habit responses and new "self-talk" Increase exposure to target group	Intervention is extremely difficult Often advisable to contain, limit or manage the behavior Very responsive to power figures Change involves issues of self-worth, trust, security, acceptance of ambiguity, and other issues Very much like a personality disorder

Addressing the Subject of Prejudice with Children

The first line of defense when addressing prejudice will always be our children. As we discussed earlier, prejudice nature is systematically ingrained in a child opposed to an adult. Parents must make it a priority to teach children of this disease. There are a number of actions that a parent can implement to address various prejudices with children. The Anti-Defamation League provides suggestions for parents concerning addressing prejudice with children. They are:

- Help your children become sensitive to other people's feelings. Talk with your children or share stories that help them understand different points of view of other people.
- Accept each of your children as unique and special. Inform your children that you recognize and appreciate their individual qualities.
- Encourage your children to construct positive change. Demonstrate how your children can respond to prejudiced acts, such as confronting a classmate's discriminatory behavior.
- Teach your children respect and an appreciation for differences by providing opportunities for interaction with people of diverse groups. Provide opportunities to learn about people through travel, books, or programs that show positive insights into other cultures.

- Make sure your children understand that prejudice and discrimination are unfair. Emphasize that no one should be teased on the basis of race ethnicity, gender, sexual orientation, appearance, or disability.
- Help children recognize instances of stereotyping, prejudice and discrimination. Discuss with your children how to respond to the above behaviors.
- Take appropriate action against prejudice and discrimination. Address the use of prejudice language when your children are present. Your children must be aware that such behavior is unacceptable even from adults.

Assessing Your Own Prejudices - Implicit Association Test

If someone asked you if you are a prejudiced person, most likely your response would be "no." In today's society, many of us strongly believe that we hold no prejudices toward certain groups or individuals. On the other end of the spectrum, there are also many individuals that believe and will admit that they are prejudiced to some extent. In order to reach a higher level of self discovery, we must consciously monitor our thinking and our surroundings in an effort to increase our sensitivity level. Self evaluation allows us to determine if we are on the correct path.

I have been guilty of prejudice a few times in my life, and I neglected to recognize my faults until I made a conscious effort toward awareness. For many years, I was primarily sensitive to ethnic/racial prejudice while omitting other forms, which are just as harmful. For example, I clearly remember a situation when I became extremely impatient and upset with an elderly man purchasing a cup of coffee at a local coffee shop. There was a delay in the purchase process and I noticed the man standing at the counter. I immediately assumed that the elderly man was the problem based solely on his age. Not for one second did I consider there could be a number of scenarios that caused the purchase delay. It could have easily been a situation where the coffee shop's employee might have caused this situation or a malfunction of the register. In addition to the unknown possibilities, I should have immediately respected the fact that he was an elder man who, based on my background, commanded immediate respect. Even though there was no verbal exchange, allowing this frustration to enter my space was truly wrong and disrespectful.

In today's society, we seem to be quite busy and preoccupied with never ending thoughts, tasks, and to-do lists. Still, we are capable of enhancing our sensitivity of prejudice within our daily routines. Understanding that fact, it would be wise to locate a resource that can provide an indication of our baseline biases. Fortunately, there are a number of tools available to provide this information. One of these tools is the Implicit Association Test (IAT). This particular test is created by Project Implicit and provides an assessment of your conscious and unconscious preferences for over 90 different topics, including ethnic groups, political issues, and even styles of music. Project Implicit is a Virtual Laboratory for the social and behavioral sciences designed to facilitate the research of implicit social cognition: cognitions, feelings, and evaluations that are not necessarily available to conscious awareness, conscious control, conscious intention, or self-reflection. Initially launched as a demonstration website in 1998 at Yale University, Project Implicit is comprised of a network of laboratories, technicians, and research scientists at Harvard University, the University of Washington, and the University of Virginia. Project Implicit is the product of research by three scientists whose work produced a new approach to understanding of attitudes, biases, and stereotypes. To experience this test, visit *https://implicit.harvard.edu/implicit/demo* and enjoy the journey. I assure you that you will not be disappointed and you may discover a few things about yourself.

Chapter Eight

Men Are Idiots!

"Terry?" Dan, Executive VP, talks into the speaker phone. "Could you call and place a lunch order for our team?"

"Yes sir. What do you have in mind?" asks Terry.

"I have a taste for sushi. Team, does Japanese sound like a winner?" asks Dan.

"Yes sir" the team responds.

"Great. Place an order for eight. We'll have ginger salad, miso soup, and shrimp tempura. We will follow the appetizer with sashimi - tuna, smoked salmon, yellow tail, white fish, mackerel, octopus, and eel. And get a number of California rolls, spicy tuna rolls, cucumber/avocado rolls, dragon rolls and salmon rolls along with a variety of drinks. Thanks, Terry."

To the group, he says, "Now let's proceed. As you all know, we are in a tough situation with this recent occurrence that has come to our attention. We understand that our product can possibly cause bodily harm to our customers in certain situations. Now what we have to determine today is this: Do we recall the current product or do we hold the recall and address the current legal issues with the affected customers? To get to our solution, let's answer some basic questions. Chris, what is the estimated cost of a major recall?" asks Dan.

As Chris reviews his spreadsheet, he responds "Well sir, our units sold over the last two years topped 10 million. In a recall situation, the cost per unit repair or replacement will be $38 with a total recall cost of $380 million."

Dan speaks again "OK, Karen, please give me a breakdown of the legal issues concerning law suits from individuals that have been affected by this situation."

"Yes sir," responds Karen, "As of today, we have a total of seven individual cases against us. The damages requested from the plaintiffs range from $1 million to $20 million with a total amount of $46 million if we settled today. Our counsel met with the attorneys of each plaintiff and they have agreed to a settlement of the current amounts."

Dan asks "Henry, what will be the public perception of the product if we make a decision to go with the recall?"

Henry responds "It will affect the public perception of our product, and sales will drop until the new version is launched next quarter."

"What were the sales over the last three years?" asks Dan.

Chris responds "Over the last three years, our annual sales percentage growth has averaged fifteen percent with a projected higher percentage based upon the new features added to the new release. Last year's revenue reached $6 billion."

"Thanks Chris. So if we can hold the number of law suits to a minimum number, settle with the existing plaintiffs provided that each settlement is contingent upon each plaintiff agreeing to a gag order, and correct the problem and move up the timetable for the next release which includes the correction, we are looking at a number far less than the recall. That's what you call a simple actuarial analysis." says Dan.

"Yes sir, Dan." Says Chris.

Dan responds "Then we will move forward with the following strategy: settle the law suits, monitor current customers concerning the existing problem until the new product release. Great work, team. Now let's enjoy lunch."

Since the beginning of time, the male species has been at the forefront of leadership, power and wealth of the majority of cultures. From controlling households, governments and religious organizations to owning the majority of the world's wealth along with defining history, societies have been framed around the patriarchy system. What is this patriarchy system? The Greek translation defines the word Patriarchy as patria (meaning father) and arche (meaning rule). Merriam-Webster defines this term as "a social organization marked by the supremacy of the father in the clan or family, the legal dependence of wives and children, and the reckoning of descent and inheritance in the male line; control by men of a disproportionately large share of power." What have men accomplished with this type of power? How has the human race evolved utilizing this system? Fortunately, a number of patriarchy systems in our past and today pursue the best for all mankind; however, there are many areas that can and must be improved for the sake of the human race.

The male species has been the controlling entity for many years and has been responsible for the majority of decisions that impact all humans. As a man, why would I write these types of things concerning men? Good question and it seems quite unusual that I would even discuss this subject. However I am sure that there are many women who would be curious of my analysis and would perhaps enjoy screaming "Men are idiots" at the top of their lungs. As a matter of fact, I think that it would be a great form of therapy for women to possibly include this verbal activity in their self discovery process. In addition, this activity should be performed in the presence of at least two men.

Throughout my adult life, I have sometimes wondered about the male's behavior and quite honestly, have been embarrassed by many of our actions and beliefs. Why would a man consciously strike or abuse a woman who is physically weaker? Why would a man make a conscious decision to cause physical, mental and/or financial harm to women, children and/or other men simply to obtain power or build wealth? Why are there politicians who create and vote on legislation that only helps to maintain their political career instead of choosing what is best for the community and their constituents? Why is there mass genocide of innocent men, women and children throughout the world? These types of questions seem to never end but should be addressed.

In this chapter, I briefly identify a number of situations along with statistics that occurred because of decisions made by a man or group of men. Each decision is characterized by either male greed, lack of consideration or compassion for the betterment of mankind or simply gross incompetence. From world hunger to corruption, there are many examples that affirm the need of improvement on our part. Eventually, our daily existence must focus on the betterment of all people opposed to the interest of a few. Let's review just a few of the situations in which men have failed.

Violence Against Women

Violence against women and girls is a major public health and human rights problem. According to the United Nations Entity for Gender Equality and the Empowerment of Women, up to 70 percent of women experience physical or sexual violence from men in their lifetime, with the majority from husbands, intimate partners or an acquaintance. This is unacceptable! Among women aged 15-44, acts of violence causes more death and disability than cancer, malaria, traffic accidents and war combined (Facts & Figures). In addition, violence against women destroys lives, families and communities. The violence to which women are subjected comes in many forms, including physical, sexual, and psychological including rape and female genital mutilation. Other practices harmful to women include sexual harassment, intimidation at work, violence related to exploitation, trafficking, and forced prostitution (Facts & Figures).

- An estimated 150 million girls under 18 suffered some form of sexual violence in 2002 alone.
- Domestic violence alone cost approximately US $1.16 billion in Canada and US $5.8 billion in the United States.
- As many as 1 in 4 women experience physical and/or sexual violence during pregnancy, which increases

the likelihood of having a miscarriage, stillbirth and abortion.

- Up to 53 percent of women physically abused by their intimate partners are being kicked or punched in the abdomen.
- In the United States, one-third of women murdered each year are killed by intimate partners.
- In South Africa, a woman is killed every 6 hours by an intimate partner. In India, 22 women were killed each day in dowry-related murders in 2007.
- Women and girls constitute 80 percent of the estimated 800,000 people trafficked annually, with the majority (79 percent) trafficked for sexual exploitation.
- Between 40 and 50 percent of women in European Union countries experience unwanted sexual advancements, physical contact or other forms of sexual harassment at their workplace.
- Approximately 250,000 to 500,000 women and girls were raped in the 1994 Rwandan genocide.
- According to "Stop Violence Against Women", in the United States, a woman is raped every six minutes and a woman is battered every 15 seconds.
- In Europe, domestic violence is the major cause of death and disability for women aged 16 to 44.

World Hunger / Poverty

Poverty is a major issue that must be swiftly addressed throughout the world. The majority of the world's people and nations are in a state of poverty. Many people live on just a few dollars a day, which leads to hunger, disease and malnutrition. The poor usually do not have a voice to make a difference, and the wealthy usually benefit from the political outcome of these types of situations. How can we solve this global problem?

According to the Food and Agriculture Organization of the United Nations (FAO), the world already produces enough food to feed every child, woman and man and could feed 12 billion people, or double the current world population (Ziegler); however, there continues to be this disconnect concerning our global system.

- The poorest 68% of the world's population accounts for 4.2% of global income. The richest 8% of world population controls 79% of total wealth (Shorrocks).
- According to UNICEF, 21,000 children die each day due to poverty (Shah). And they "die quietly in some of the poorest villages on earth, far removed from the scrutiny and the conscience of the world. Being meek and weak in life makes these dying multitudes even more invisible in death."
- At least 80% of humanity lives on less than $10 a day.

- According to the United Nations Food and Agriculture Organization, 1.02 billion people are undernourished; children are the most visible victims of this situation.

Female Genital Mutilation

Female Genital Mutilation (FGM), or Female Genital Cutting (FGC), is defined as a procedure that intentionally alters female genital organs for non-medical reasons and offers no health benefits for girls and women. According to the World Health Organization (WHO), there are an estimated 100 to 140 million girls and women worldwide living with the consequences of FGM. This is recognized by many world organizations as a violation of the human rights of girls and women internationally. Along with many knowing this procedure demonstrates inequality between men and women and triggers a list of short and long term consequences, the process is performed mainly on young girls between infancy and age 15. FGM is often practiced based upon cultural beliefs. Many believe that this process inspires submissiveness in young women, reduces a woman's desire for sex and signifies the acceptance of a woman into society.

In 1997, The World Health Organization issued a joint statement against the practice of FGM. Joining organizations included United Nations Population Fund (UNFPA) and United Nations Children's Fund (UNICEF). In 2008, with increased support, WHO issued a new statement stressing the abandonment of FGM based upon new evidence which included the above data along with research concerning the damaging effects.

September 11th Attacks (9/11)

The September 11, 2001 attacks were a number of coordinated suicide attacks upon the United States by Al Qaeda. On that day, four commercial passenger airliners were hijacked. Two of the airliners, American Airlines Flight 11 and United Airlines Flight 175, were intentionally crashed into the South and North Towers of the World Trade Center complex in New York City. American Airlines Flight 77 was intentionally crashed into the Pentagon, and hijackers of United Airlines Flight 93 crashed into an empty field in Shanksville, Pennsylvania. As a result of the attacks, 2,976 victims lost their lives. There were 246 victims on the four planes, 2605 victims in and around the North and South Towers and 125 victims at the Pentagon.

Trans-Atlantic Slave Trade

Beginning in the 15th century and lasting for more than three centuries, the trans-atlantic slave trade was implemented by European empires, such as Portugal and

Spain. The primary interest was labor, and African men, women, and children were enslaved and transported to colonies of the New World. The enslaved people were extracted mainly from West and Central Africa and taken to North and South American destinations to provide free labor creating an enormous amount of wealth for Europe and America. A number of scholars have estimated that there were twelve million Africans extracted and imported to various European colonies including a large number who actually died during the voyages (United Nations).

The Holocaust

The Holocaust was a systematic extermination of six million people of the Jewish population orchestrated by Adolph Hitler and Nazi Germany. According to the United States Holocaust Memorial Museum, in 1933 the Jewish population of Europe totaled over nine million people. By 1945, the Germans killed close to two out of every three European Jews as part of Nazi policies. Beginning with legislation to remove the Jews from civil society, the process continued with the implementation of concentration camps and mass shootings to gas chambers to kill Jews. There were a number of other groups that were targeted by the German authorities during this era, including the disabled, Slavic peoples, Gypsies, Socialists, and homosexuals.

German justification was based upon what they considered racial inferiority.

Hurricane Katrina

In August of 2005, Hurricane Katrina hit the southern coast of the United States and was one of the deadliest and costliest hurricanes in the history of the United States. More than 1,800 people lost their lives during the hurricane, and subsequent flooding and damages totaled over $100 billion. Thousands of residents were trapped in New Orleans without sufficient food, water or medical care and many were displaced to many states. The flooding occurred because of failure of the levee designed, constructed and maintained by the US Army Corps of Engineers (USACE) and the lack of timely responses from the Federal Emergency Management Agency (FEMA), state and local governments. The lack of a timely response resulted in the firing of FEMA Director Michael Brown and New Orleans Police Department Superintendant Eddie Compass. An investigation was launched and the court ruled that the Army Corps of Engineers' gross mismanagement of maintenance at the Mississippi River-Gulf Outlet was directly responsible for flood damage in St. Bernard Parish and the Lower 9th Ward.

BP Oil Spill

In 2010, BP global revenue reached $297 billion; however, research has determined that BP declined to install a certain technology on their deep water oil drilling rig that would have prevented the oil spill in the Gulf. The decision not to use the safe technology was based upon, of course, saving money, about $7 million. Because of this oil spill, tourism in many areas in the Gulf has reduced drastically, many business owners have either lost their businesses or suffered a drastic reduction in overall revenue.

Genocide

In 1948, the United Nations defined genocide as any of the following acts committed with intent to destroy, in whole or in part, a national, ethnical, racial or religious group: (a) killing members of the group; (b) causing serious bodily or mental harm to members of the group; (c) deliberately inflicting on the group conditions of life calculated to bring about its physical destruction in whole or in part; (d) imposing measures intended to prevent births within the group; (e) forcibly transferring children of the group to another group. The term genocide was defined in 1944 by the Polish lawyer Raphael Lemkin, who combined the Greek word genos (race) with the Latin word cide (to kill). There have been a number of past occurrences such as:

Stalin's Forced Famine – 7,000,000 Deaths (1932-1933)

Nazi Holocaust - 6,000,000 Deaths (1938-1945)

Native American – 10,000,000 Deaths

Pol Pot in Cambodia – 2,000,000 Deaths (1975-1979)

Armenians in Turkey – 1,500,000 Deaths (1915-1918)

Rwanda – 800,000 Deaths (1994)

Darfur War – 300,000 Deaths (2003-Present)

Bosnia-Herzegovina – 200,000 Deaths (1992-1995)

Darfur War - The conflict in Darfur, Sudan, began in February 2003 when the Justice and Equality Movement and the Sudan Liberation Army in Darfur launched attacks against the government to fight against the political and economic marginalization of Darfur. Sudan, Africa's largest country, is located south of Egypt. The Darfur region is an area of western Sudan roughly the size of Texas, with a population of approximately 6 million people before the crisis. Through military raids, the Sudanese military specifically targeted ethnic groups that provided support for the Sudan People's Liberation Movement/Army. Throughout this war, hundreds of thousands of civilians have been killed and over 400 villages were completely destroyed. The United Nations estimates the death toll to be over 300,000. Up to 2.5 million Darfuris have fled their homes and continue to live in camps throughout Darfur or in refugee camps in the Central African Republic and Chad.

Corporate Fraud

Enron Scandal – The Enron scandal of 2001 resulted from accounting loopholes and poor financial reporting to hide billions in debt from failed deals and projects. The corporate scandal led to the largest bankruptcy in American history at that time. Enron executives, including Chief Executive Officer Kenneth Lay and Chief Financial Officer Andrew Fastow, misled Enron's audit committee and board of directors on high-risk accounting issues. The scandal also led to the fall of Arthur Andersen, which was one of the five largest accounting firms in the world. With a stock price of $90 per share in 2000, Enron's stock price dropped to less than a $1 by November 2001, causing shareholders to lose nearly $11 billion. At that time, the U.S. Securities and Exchange Commission (SEC) began an investigation. Enron filed for bankruptcy in December 2001. Many Enron executives were indicted for a number of charges and later sentenced to prison. Arthur Andersen, Enron's auditor, seized operations which cost employees and shareholders billions in stock prices and pensions.

AIG (American International Group) – Operating as one of the largest insurance companies, AIG offers many types of insurance worldwide. In 2007, the AIG assets exceeded one trillion dollars. In 2008, the company was unable to meet payments on many contracts which should have led to bankruptcy. But AIG never filed for bankruptcy. The federal government stepped in and supplied AIG with the necessary funds to continue operations. AIG took unprecedented risk which lead to a government bailout totaling over $150 billion in taxpayer money. After receiving valued taxpayer funds, AIG continued to distribute over $165 million in bonus payouts. Along with the taxpayer bailout, the stockholders of AIG lost most of their investment in the company. In 2000, the AIG stock reached $104 a share dropping to under $2 a share in 2008. During 2006 and 2007, many company insiders sold AIG stock heavily. Between 2000 and 2006, the company engaged in a number of frauds. These different frauds lead to criminal and civil prosecutions and convictions of AIG officers.

WorldCom – Between 1999 and 2002, WorldCom executives engaged in accounting fraud to hide its declining financial condition. False claims of financial growth and profitability in order to increase the price of the company's stock led to one of the largest bankruptcy cases in history. The first illegal activity, consisting of approximately $3.8 billion of fraud, was discovered by WorldCom's internal audit department. Scott Sullivan, CFO, told company employees to falsify the accounting and auditing documents and also lied in public statements concerning WorldCom. Sullivan was fired, and the Securities and Exchange Commission launched an investigation. By the fourth quarter of 2003, the company's total assets had been inflated to close to $11 billion. The scam also included Chief Executive Officer Bernard Ebbers, who capitalized on WorldCom stocks that fell and then received corporate loans and guarantees totaling more than $400 million that were never repaid.

Investment Scandals

Bernard L. Madoff – The Madoff investment scandal was a ponzi scheme implemented by Bernard Madoff, who founded Bernard L. Madoff Investment Securities LLC in 1960. Madoff defrauded 4,800 investors of an estimated $65 billion. He admitted that since 1996, he ceased trading on the market and fabricated investors' returns. In 2009, he was sentenced to 150 years in prison. Investigators have determined that others were also involved in the ponzi scheme. Madoff's longtime accountant, David G. Friehling, plead guilty to deliberately producing audits that helped to conceal Madoff's enormous Ponzi scheme from regulators for 20 years. The Madoff ponzi scheme forced major losses to individuals and charities.

Marc Dreier – Labeled "the Houdini of impersonation and false documents," Marc Dreier swindled more than $700 million in financial assets from a number of investors. Between 2004 and 2008, Dreier, a prominent Manhattan attorney, defrauded a number of hedge funds, investment funds and individual investors by selling fictitious securities. Dreier plead guilty to charges of money laundering, conspiracy, securities fraud and wire fraud and received a prison sentence of 25 years.

Exploitation Colonialism

For thousands of years, colonialism has been in existence, transforming and manipulating entire societies to satisfy the needs of colonial rulers or governments. The book, Colonialism: A Theoretical Overview (Osterhammel) defines colonialism simply as "a relationship of domination between an indigenous (or foreign imported) majority and a minority of foreign invaders. The fundamental decisions affecting the lives of the colonized people are made and implemented by the colonial rulers in pursuit of interests that are often defined in a distant metropolis. Rejecting cultural compromises with the colonized population, the colonizers are convinced of their own superiority and of their ordained mandate to rule." According to historians, there are two forms of colonialism: Settler Colonialism and Exploitation Colonialism. Settler Colonialism consists of a large number of colonists, typically seeking fertile land to farm. Exploitation colonialism usually involved a smaller number of colonists usually interested in extracting resources to export to the metropole (Mother City, Mother Country). An example of exploitation colonialism would be the Age of Discovery. The Age of Discovery began in the 15th century and continued into the 17th century involving European exploration throughout Africa, Asia and the Americas.

I completely understand that the items listed above are just the tip of the iceberg concerning unscrupulous actions of men. As a man, I apologize. However, please hold us accountable for our actions!

Excuses are monuments of nothingness.
They build bridges to nowhere.
Those that use these tools of incompetence
are masters of nothingness.

Anonymous

Bibliography

Adams, Lon. "Is It Okay to Choose Childlessness?" 2006. Christianity.com. Web. August 2010. <www.christianity.com>.

Agrillo, Christian and Nelini, Cristian. "Childfree by choice: a review." *Journal of Cultural Geography*, Vol. 25, No. 3, October 2008. EBSCO. Web. June 2011.

Allport, G.W. *The Nature of Prejudice 25th Anniversary Edition*. 1979. New York, NY: Basic Books/Perseus Books Group, 2011. Print.

"America's Children: Key National Indicators of Well-Being, 2011." *Federal Interagency Forum on Child and Family Statistics 2011*. Web. August 2011. <www.childstats.gov>.

American Society of Plastic Surgeons Report of the 2010 Plastic Surgery Statistics. ASPS National Clearinghouse of Plastic Surgery Procedural Statistics, 2010. Print.

"American Time Use Survey 2003." *Bureau of Labor Statistics, U.S. Department of Labor 2003*. Web. June 2010.

Anti-Defamation League. "What to Tell Your Child About Prejudice and Discrimination: What Can Parents Do about Prejudice?" 2001. *Anti-Defamation League*. 2001. Web. June 2011. < www.adl.org>.

Arendell, Teresa. "Soccer Moms' and the New Care Work 2000." *University of California, Berkeley: Sloan Center for Working Parents*. Web. May 2010. <http://wfnetwork.bc.edu/berkeley/papers/16.pdf>.

Bennett, Judith M., Clark, Elizabeth A., and O'Barr, Jean F., eds. *Sisters and Workers in the Middle Ages*. Chicago: University of Chicago Press, 1989. Print.

Berelson, Bernard. "The Value of Children: Taxonomical Essay." *Population Council Annual Report*, 1972. New York, Population Council.

Bianchi, Suzanne and Casper, Lynne M. "American Families." *Population Bulletin*. Vol. 55, No. 4, December 2000. Population Reference Bureau. Web. August 2010. <http://www.prb.org/pdf/55.4AmericanFamilies.pdf >.

Bianchi, Suzanne M., Robinson, John P., and Milkie, Melissa A. *Changing Rhythms of American Family Life*. New York: Russell Sage Foundation, 2006. Print.

Bochner, S. (1986), "Coping with Unfamiliar cultures: adjustment or culture learning?." *Australian Journal of Psychology*, 38: 347-358. doi: 10.1080/00049538608259021.

Bond, Marybeth. "Women Travel Statistics-The Latest 2010." *Gutsy Traveler*, 2010. Web. February 2011. <www.gutsytraveler.com>.

Brenner, Helene G., and Letich, Laurence. *I Know I'm in There Somewhere: A Woman's Guide to Finding Her Inner Voice*. New York, NY: Gotham Books, 2003. Print.

"Bridal Shower History: The Legend of the Bridal Shower." 2011. *Bridal-Showers.net*. Web.. July 2011. <www.bridal-showers.net>.

Brickman, P., Coates, D., and Janoff-Bulman, R. "Lottery Winners and Accident Victims: Is Happiness Relative?" 1978. *Journal of Personality and Social Psychology*, Web. July 2011. <www.psychnet.apa.org>.

Britt, Robert. "Cosmetic Surgery Expected to Soar, June 2008." *TechMediaNetwork* 2010. Web. June 2010. <www.livescience.com/7522-cosmetic-surgery-expected-soar.html>.

Brooks, Cindy. 'Wedding History 101: Flower Girl Customs & Traditions." April 5, 2010. *The Brass Paperclip Project*, 2011. Web. August 2011. <www.brasspaperclip.typepad.com>.

"Careerbuilder.com Survey." 2005. *Kiplinger's Personal Finance*, December 2005. Web. May, 2011.

Casey, Terri. *Pride and Joy: The Lives and Passions of Women Without Children.* New York, NY: Simon & Schuster, 1998. Print.

Clark, Kenneth and Clark, Mamie. "Emotional Factors in Racial Identification and Preference in Negro Children." 1950. *The Journal of Negro Education*, Vol. 19, No. 3. The Negro Child in the American Social Order 1950.

Cole, Jim, Ed.D. "Understanding Prejudice." *Beyond Prejudice: Understanding Prejudicial Behavior*. 2011. Web. March 2011. < www.beyondprejudice.com>.

"Colonialism." *Wikipedia*. Web. July 2011.

"Convention on the Prevention and Punishment of the Crime of Genocide 1948. General Assembly Resolution 260." *United Nations*. Web. August 2011. < www.preventgenocide.org>.

Coontz, Stephanie. *Marriage, a History: From Obedience to Intimacy, How Love Conquered Marriage.* New York, NY: Penguin Group, 2005. Print.

"Cosmetic Surgery Markets: Products and Services: Report Highlights." *BCC Research* July 2009. Web. ReportLinker. July 2011. <www.reportlinker.com/p0132720/Cosmetic-Surgery-Markets-Products-and-Services.html>.

Crotts, John C., Mason, Peyton R., and Davis, Boyd. "Measuring Guest Satisfaction and Competitive Position in the Hospitality and Tourism Industry: An Application of Stance-Shift Analysis to Travel Blog Narratives." *Journal of Travel Research*, Nov 2009; vol.48. Print.

Diener, Ed, Horwitz, Jeff, and Emmons, Robert A. "Happiness of the Very Wealthy," 1985. *Social Indicators Research*, Vol. 16, Number 3, 263-274. Web. June 2011. <www.generallythinking.com>.

Dorr, Gregory Michael. "Racial Integrity Laws of the 1920s." *Encyclopedia Virginia*. Ed. Brendan Wolfe. 20 May, 2011. Virginia Foundation for the Humanities. 7 Apr. 2011. <www.EncyclopediaVirginia.org/Racial_Integrity_Laws_of_the_1920s>.

"Dowry." *Women's Health Encyclopedia*. 2011. Web. September 2011.

Dragon, Debbie. "History of Wedding Flowers." *LoveToKnow*, 2011. Web. August 2011. <http://weddings.lovetoknow.com>.

Dweck, Carol S., Lewis and Virginia Eaton Professor, *Stanford University: Department of Psychology.*

Etcoff, Nancy. *Survival of the Prettiest: The Science of Beauty.* New York, NY: Anchor Publisher, 1999. Print.

"Facts & Figures on VAW 2011." *UN Entity for Gender Equality and the Empowerment of Women 2011*. Web. August 2011.

Frederick, Shane and Lowenstein, George. 1999. Hedonic adaptation. In E. Jahneman, E. Diener and N. Schwartz (eds), *Well-being: The Foundations of Hedonic Psychology* (pp. 302-29). New York: Russell Sage Foundation.

Gardner, Howard. *Frames of Mind: The Theory of Multiple Intelligences.* New York, NY: BasicBooks, 1993. Questia. Web. July 2011. <www.questia.com>.

Gray, Madeleine. *The Protestant Reformation: belief, practice, and tradition.* Eastbourne, East Sussex, UK: Sussex Academic Press, 2003. Print.

Halsall, Paul. "Medieval Sourcebook: Twelfth Ecumenical Council: Lateran IV 1215: The Canons of the Fourth Lateran Council, 1215." New York, NY: Fordham University. Web. July 2011. <www.fordham.edu>.

"Happiness." *Merriam-Webster.com*, 2011. Web. April 2011.

"Health." *World Health Organization*, 1946. Web. Wikipedia, 2011. <http://en.wikipedia.org/wiki/Health. December 2010>.

"Hedonic Treadmill." *PsychWiki – A Collaborative Psychology Wiki.* June 2010. Web. August 2010.

Herman, Roger, and Gioia, Joyce. "The Herman Trend Alert 2007." The Herman Group. 2011. Web. March 2011. < www.hermangroup.com>.

HGP. "An Overview of the Human Genome Project." *National Human Genome Research Institute: National Institutes of Health*, 2011. Web. May 2011. < www.genome.gov>.

"Implicit Association Test." *Project Implicit*, 2011. Web. January 2011. <http://implicit.harvard.edu>.

"Introduction to the Holocaust." *United States Holocaust Memorial Museum*, 2011. Web. September 2011. <www.ushmm.org>.

Jaworski, Adam, and Galasinski, Dariusz. "Representations of Hosts in Travel Writing 2003." *The Guardian Travel*, Section Vol. 1, No. 2, 2003. Web. May 2011. <www.cf.ac.uk>.

Jaworski, Adam. Ylänne-McEwen, V., Thurlow, C. and Lawson, S. (2003), "Social roles and negotiation of status in host-tourist interaction: A view from British television holiday programmes." *Journal of Sociolinguistics*, 7: 135-164. doi: 10.1111/1467-9481.00217.

Karam, M. "History of the Wedding Ring." *LoveToKnow*, 2011. Web. August 2011. <http://weddings.lovetoknow.com>.

"Kidnapping the Bride: Best Man History 2011." *Best Man Survival Guide: How to Survive the Best Man Duties and Speech*, 2011. Web. July 2011. <www.best-man-survival-guide.com>.

Krautter, Ken. *Our Republic Walk*,2011. Web. January, 2011. <www.kenkrautter.net>.

Kugel, Seth. "The Gender Gap in Travel: Myths and Revelations.". *The New York Times*, September 6, 2011. Web. September 2011. < http://frugaltraveler.blogs.nytimes.com>.

Lino, Mark. "Expenditures on Children by Families, 2010." *U.S. Department of Agriculture, Center for Nutrition Policy and Promotion*, 2011. Miscellaneous Publication No. 1528-2010.

Livingston, Gretchen and Cohn, D'Vera. "Childlessness Up Among All Women; Down Among Women with Advanced Degrees 2010." *Pew Research Center*. Web. April 2011. <www.pewsocialtrends.org>.

Lyubomirsky, Sonja. *How of Happiness: A Scientific Approach to Getting the Life You Want*. 2007. New York: The Penguin Press, 2007. Print.

Marketing to Women. "Hotels attempt to attract women travelers through amenities, value-adds, and, naturally, low prices." *EPM Communications, Inc.*,2009. Web. HighBeam Research. May 2011. <www.highbeam.com>.

Martin, Thomas. R. *Ancient Greece: From Prehistoric to Hellenistic Times*. New Haven, MA: Yale University Press, 2000. Print.

Mlambo-Ngcuka, Phumzile. 4th Annual Women's Parliament Conference, Cape Town, Africa, August 2007. Web. Anzia, Lys. "Educate a Woman, You Educate a Nation" – South Africa Aims to Improve its Education for Girls." *Women News Network*. August 2007. Web. July 2011. <www.womensnewsnetwork.net>.

Mohler, Albert. "Deliberate Childlessness: Moral Rebellion With a New Face." 2005. Web. June 2010. <www.albertmohler.com>.

Myers, David G., "The Pursuit of Happiness, Discovering the Pathway to Fulfillment, Well-Being, and Enduring Personal Joy." 1992. New York, NY: HarperCollins Publishers, 1992. December, 2010. Print.

Myers, David G. "Wealth, Well-being, and the New American Dream." *Hope College*. 2007. Web. May 2011. www.davidmyers.org>.

"National Survey of Family Growth 2008." *National Center for Health Statistics, Center for Disease Control*. Web. May 2010.

Okun, Lewis. *Woman Abuse: facts replacing myths*. Albany, NY: State University of New York Press Albany, 1986. Print.

Osterhammel, Jurgen and Frisch, Shelley. *Colonialism: A Theoretical Overview 2005*. Princeton, NJ: Markus Wiener Publishers, 2005. December 2010. Print.

Paul, Richard. "Critical Thinking: Basic Questions and Answers." *Foundation for Critical Thinking*. The Center for Critical Thinking, 2010. Web. November 2010. <www.criticalthinking.org/pages/critical-thinking-basic-questions-amp-answers/409>.

Paul, Richard, and Elder, Linda. "Becoming a Critic of Your Thinking." *Foundation for Critical Thinking*. The Center for Critical Thinking, 2011. Web. February 2011. <www.criticalthinking.org/pages/becoming-a-critic-of-your-thinking/478>.

Paul, Richard, and Elder, Linda. "Critical Thinking Development: A Stage Theory, 2010." *Foundation for Critical Thinking*. The Center for Critical Thinking, 2011. Web. May 2011. <www.criticalthinking.org/pages/critical-thinking-development-a-stage-theory/483>.

Paul, Richard, and Elder, Linda. "Critical Thinking in Everyday Life: 9 Strategies, 2001." *Foundation for Critical Thinking*. The Center for Critical Thinking, 2010. Web. October 2010. <www.criticalthinking.org>.

Paul, Richard, and Elder, Linda. "The Miniature Guide to Critical Thinking Concepts and Tools, 2006." *Foundation for Critical Thinking.* The Center for Critical Thinking, 2011. Web. February 2011. <www.criticalthinking.org/files/Concepts_Tools.pdf>.

Paul, Richard, and Elder, Linda. *The Thinker's Guide to the Art of Strategic Thinking: 25 Weeks to Better Thinking and Better Living.* Dillion Beach, CA: Foundation for Critical Thinking, 2004. Print.

Paul, Richard, and Scriven, Michael. "Defining Critical Thinking." *Foundation for Critical Thinking.* The Center for Critical Thinking, 2011. Web. February 2011. <www.criticalthinking.org/pages/defining-critical-thinking/410>.

Perrone, Ed. "Age of Aquarius: A New Age Dawning, 2005." *InnerSelf 2010.* Web. August 2010. <innerself.com/content/articles/personal-growth/astrology/general/4374-age-of-aquarius-a-new-age-dawning.html>.

Peterson, Ann-Kristin, and Rohrer, Jürg. "Definition of intuition" *Time for Change,* 2011. Web. March 2011. <http://timeforchange.org/definition-of-intuition-intuitive>.

Peterson, Christopher, and Seligman, Martin. "Character Strengths and Virtues: A Handbook and Classification, 2004." *VIA Institute on Character.* New York: Oxford University Press, Web. November 2010. < www.viacharacter.org>.

Phillippe, F.L., Vallerand, R.J. and Lavigne, G.L. 2009, "Passion Does Make a Difference in People's Lives: A Look at Well-Being in Passionate and Non-Passionate Individuals." *Applied Psychology: Health and Well-Being,* 1:3-22. doi:10.1111/j.1758-0854.2008.01003.x. Web. Wiley Online Library. August 2011.

Psychology Wiki. "Intercultural Communication Principles." *Wikia, Inc.,* 2011. Web. December 2010.

Queen Afua. *Sacred Woman: A Guide to Healing the Feminine Body, Mind, and Spirit.* New York, NY: Random House Publishing Group, 2001. Print.

Roney, Carley. "Wedding Traditions: Meaning of "Something Old, Something New..." *The Knot,* 2011. Web. September 2011. <http://wedding.theknot.com>.

Scott, Elizabeth. "The Stress Management and Health Benefits of Laughter." January 2011. *About.com Stress Management.* 2011. Web. April 2011. <http://stress.about.com/od/stresshealth/a/laughter.htm>.

Seligman, Martin E.P. *Authentic Happiness: Using the New Positive Psychology to Realize Your Potential for Lasting Fulfillment.* New York: The Free Press, 2003. Print.

Seligman, Martin E.P. *The Positive Psychology Center. University of Pennsylvania, 2011.* Web. February 2011. <www.ppc.sas.upenn.edu>.

Seligman, Martin E.P., and Csikszentmihalyi, Mihaly 2000. "Positive Psychology: An Introduction." *American Psychologist* 55 (1): 5-14. Web. May 2010. <www.generallythinking.com>.

Shah, Anup. "Today, around 21,000 children died around the world." *Global Issues: Social, Political, Economic and Environmental Issues That Affect Us All.* Web. September 2011. <www.globalissues.org>.

Shaw, George Bernard, Quote. "Back to Methuselah: 1921." part 1, act 1.

Shea, John B. "Having or not having children." *Catholic Insight*. September 2009 Issue. Web. July 2010. <www.catholicinsight.com>.

Shorrocks, A., Davies, J., and Lluberas, R. "The Wealth Pyramid, Global Wealth Report 2010." *Credit Suisse Research Institute*. Web. April 2011.

Sihera, Elaine. "The Sihera Confidence Guide." *The Sihera Relationship Guide*, 2011. Web. December 2010. <www.elainesden.org>.

"Six Pillars of Character." *Josephson Institute*, 2011. Web. April 2011. <www.josephsoninstitute.org/sixpillars.html>.

Smith, Julianne. "Wedding Garter History 2009." *The Garter Girl*. Web. June 2011. <www.thegartergirl.com>.

Smith, Melinda, Kemp, Gina, and Segal, Jeanne. "Laughter is the Best Medicine, The Health Benefits of Humor and Laughter." *Helpguide*. 2011. Web. March 2011. <http://www.helpguide.org/life/humor_laughter_health.htm>.

Smith, Dr. Robin L. National television personality, best selling author, ordained minister, keynote speaker, and licensed psychologist. September 2011. <www.drrobinsmith.com>.

Stevenson, Betsey, and Wolfers, Justin. "The Paradox of Declining Female Happiness." *American Economic Journal: Economic Policy*. 2009, 1:2, 190-225. Web. November 2010.

Taylor, Paul, Fry, Richard, and Cohn, D'Vera. "Women, Men and the New Economics of Marriage." January 19, 2010. Washington, DC: *Pew Research Center: Pew Social & Demographic Trends Project*. Web. May 2011. <www.pewsocialtrends.org>.

Taylor, Paul, Funk, Cary, and Clark, April. "As Marriage and Parenthood Drift Apart, Public Is Concerned about Social Impact 2007." *Pew Research Center*. Web. May 2010.

Teele, Sue. "The relationship of multiple intelligences to the instructional process, curriculum and instruction, Unpublished Dissertation, University of California Riverside, 1994. Web.

Tejada-Vera B, Sutton PD. "Births, Marriages, Divorces, and Deaths: Provisional Data for 2009." *National Vital Statistics Reports. vol 58, no 25.* Hyattsville, MD: National Center for Health Statistics. Web. May 2011.

"The Condition of Education 2011." *U.S. Department of Education, National Center for Education Statistics* 2011. Web. August 2011.

"The Millennium Development Goals Report 2011." June 2011, ISBN 978-92-1-101244-6. United Nations. Web. September 2011. <www.unhcr.org/refworld/docid/4e42118b2.html>.

Thompson, James C. "Women and Marriage in Ancient Rome." 2010. *Women in the Ancient World*. 2010. Web. June 2011.

"Trends in Childlessness Among Women by Cohort." *Organisation for Economic Co-operation and Development*, 2005. Web. August 2010.

Tucker, Abigail. "Food & Think: The Strange History of the Wedding Cake." July 13, 2009. *Smithsonian Magazine*. Web. May 2011. <http://blogs.smithsonianmag.com>.

UN Children's Fund (UNICEF). "Adolescence, an Age of Opportunity: The State of the World's Children 2011." February 2011, ISBN: 978-92-806-4555-2. Web. September 2011. <http://www.unhcr.org/refworld/docid/4d6cfa162.html>.

United Nations. "Female General Mutilation." Fact Sheet No. 241, February 2010. *World Health Organization: United Nations*, 2011. Web. August 2011. <www.who.int>.

United Nations. "International Day of Remembrance of the Victims of Slavery and the Transatlantic Slave Trade, Fact Sheet: Slavery Today 2008." *United Nations*. Web. July 2011.

"U.S. Census Bureau, 2010 Census." *U.S. Department of Commerce*. 2010. Web. July 2011. <www.census.gov>.

Vallerand, Robert J. "On the Psychology of Passion: In Search of What Makes People's Lives Most Worth Living." *Canadian Psychology*, Vol. 49, Nbr. 1, 2008. ProQuest. Web. August 2011.

"Violence Against Women." *UN Entity for Gender Equality and the Empowerment of Women 2011*. Web. August 2011. <www.unwomen.org>.

Waterworth, J. Ed. and trans. 1848. "The Council of Trent: The Canons and Decrees of the Sacred and Oecumenical Council of Trent." *Hanover Historical Texts Project*, 2011. Hanover, IN: Hanover College: History Department, Web. July 2011. <http://history.hanover.edu/texts/trent.html>.

"Wedding Rings and Engagement Rings History." *Engagement Rings History*, 2011. Web. August 2011. <www.engagementringshistory.com>.

Winfrey, Oprah. Web. BrainyQuote.com. Xplore Inc, 2011. August 2011. <www.brainyquote.com/quotes/o/oprahwinfr386189.html>.

Wolf, Naomi. *The Beauty Myth: How Images of Beauty Are Used Against Women*. New York: Harper Collins Publishers, 2002. Print.

World Bank. "World Development Indicators." *World Bank*, July 2011. Web. August 2011.

World Tourism Organization (UNWTO/OMT). *United Nations*, 2011. Web. February 2011.

World Tourism Organization. "1st trend: Tourism is constantly-growing." *United Nations*. Web. July 2011.

World Tourism Organization. "UNWTO Tourism Highlights 2011 Edition." *United Nations*, 2011. Web. September 2011.

"Women's Statistics." *Girlpower Marketing, Strategic Marketing to the Intelligent Woman*, 2011. Web. September 2011. <www.girlpowermarketing.com/women_statistics.html>.

Ziegler, J. "Economic, Social and Cultural Rights: The Right to Food 2000." *United Nations - Economic and Social Council: Commission on Human Rights, Fifty-seventh session 2001*. Web. July 2011.

Index

www.ingramcontent.com/pod-product-compliance
Lightning Source LLC
Chambersburg PA
CBHW031549300426
44111CB00006BA/236

* 9 7 8 0 6 1 5 4 6 5 9 2 0 *